Praise for *Grace & Mercy*

"*Grace & Mercy* presents an honest, encouraging look at life with its disquieting issues. Katie welcomed me to sit beside her "knee to knee" with Jesus, the Wonderful Counselor, then to journey onward, with Him leading the way."
—Chuck Rizer, Lieutenant Colonel, Army Chaplain (retired) and author of *Downwind of Thunder*

"This devotional is wonderfully refreshing and special. I love the practical, chatty, relatable style that makes recognizing God's presence and love in our lives so accessible. If you want to benefit from experiencing God in your everyday life, *Grace & Mercy* is for you."
—Rob Davis, Founding Pastor, Vineyard Church, Hopkinton Massachusetts

"*Grace & Mercy* makes faith come alive. A perfect book for a book club! The writing is fresh, candid, and detailed. The stories bring the ins and outs of an ordinary life to the surface. The tensions of walking in faith by the Spirit of God are expressed with such honesty. The conversation starters for each chapter are sure to lead to meaningful discussions in any group setting."
—Milagros Moore, Evangelist, CREDO Minister, Hagerstown, Maryland

"My wife, Beth, is often suggesting daily devotionals for me. Out of respect for her and a desire to move closer to God, I try. I just can't get into them. She was surprised to see me devouring *Grace & Mercy* and asked, 'What's different about this one?' I paused a moment, looked up and said, 'I can relate to these. Let's gather some friends and dig into it.' *Grace & Mercy* provides an interesting and engaging tool to study the Bible."
—Jim Lenaway, Pastor, B-Free Church, Bradford, Pennsylvania

"Pictures and stories and memories are three of God's sweet gifts to help us visualize his truths and strengthen our hearts. Katie and Chris use all of these to paint little portraits that add color and depth to how I understand and experience God."

—Kirk Freeman, Lead Pastor,
CrossBridge Community Church, San Antonio, Texas

"When I read selections from *Grace & Mercy*, I remembered Pastor Chris's sermons and was excited to hear how they affected Ms. Katie. This book shows how the pastor's message from a Sunday or Wednesday can change our hearts and minds. It reminds me to take sermon notes and think about what message is preached each week. Teenagers will enjoy this book!"

—Harrison Doyle, high school student,
Ablaze: Student Staff, San Antonio, Texas

"Pastors, *Grace & Mercy* is a must read. Every pastor, minister, and Christian speaker would be affirmed, encouraged, and educated if they could be exposed to honest thoughts about their messages, from someone willing to listen well and write down what they have learned. Everybody in a church congregation should read this book – not only to be personally inspired, but to be encouraged to write down the gleanings from your own pastors' sermons. What a wonderful way to bless the one who breaks bread with you!

Anyone discouraged about Christianity, or disappointed because of a church experience, should read this book. It will renew your faith and hope in what God is doing elsewhere. Perhaps it could stir up a new work in you. Small groups should read this book as a study, since the content and study guide questions are so helpful, practical, and on target. Last of all, if you just want a fun story and be inspired by the journey of one woman's experience as a mom, wife, doctor and lover of God, this book is for you. Katie Yancosek has crammed more than three lifetimes worth of experiences into one and writes about them in a fun, refreshing, and compelling way."

—Joe Castillo, Artist, Pastor, Speaker, and
author of *Sandstory* and *The Face of Christ*

a

Grace & Mercy

A DEVOTIONAL JOURNEY

KATHLEEN YANCOSEK and CHRIS DILLASHAW

Loving Healing Press
Ann Arbor, MI

Grace & Mercy: a devotional journey
Copyright © 2021 by Kathleen Yancosek and Chris Dillashaw. All Rights Reserved.
2nd Printing – March 2021

Published by   Distributed by: Ingram (USA/CAN)
Loving Healing Press   and Bertram's Books (UK/EU)
5145 Pontiac Trail
Ann Arbor, MI 48105

info@LHPress.com   Tollfree 888-761-6268
www.LHPress.com   FAX 734-663-6861

Library of Congress Cataloging-in-Publication Data

Names: Yancosek, Kathleen, 1975- author. | Dillashaw, Chris, 1974- author.
Title: Grace & mercy : a devotional journey / Kathleen Yancosek and Chris Dillashaw.
Other titles: Grace and mercy
Description: Ann Arbor, MI : Loving Healing Press, [2021] | Includes bibliographical references and index. | Summary: "Through a series of lessons based both on life experiences and Christian scripture, the authors provide a framework for addressing personal, professional, and spiritual issues in life and family settings. Includes exercises for the reader"-- Provided by publisher.
Identifiers: LCCN 2021000466 (print) | LCCN 2021000467 (ebook) | ISBN 9781615995592 (paperback) | ISBN 9781615995608 (hardcover) | ISBN 9781615995615 (epub) | ISBN 9781615995615 (ebook)
Subjects: LCSH: Devotional literature.
Classification: LCC BV4801 .Y36 2021 (print) | LCC BV4801 (ebook) | DDC 242--dc23
LC record available at https://lccn.loc.gov/2021000466
LC ebook record available at https://lccn.loc.gov/2021000467

Contents

A Note from Katie

I want to thank several pastors. I am grateful for being (or having been) a well-cared for sheep in their flocks, following in their footsteps as they walked closely behind the Good Shepherd. You will meet Pastor Chris in this book, and I want to thank him most of all! Through Chris' ministry, God restored the years the locusts had eaten in my life. My other pastors at CrossBridge Community Church have blessed me in countless ways. They are Kirk Freeman, Brian Hannas, Matt Erbaugh, Andrew Fillingim, Bryan McCleery, and Shawn Sullivan. When I lived in Kentucky, Pastor Joe Castillo taught me to live from the heart. He also baptized me and my oldest son, Joshua. When I lived in Massachusetts, Pastor Rob Davis showed me how to live a life led by the faithful, truth-revealing Spirit of God.

I served in the U.S. Army for twenty years and received superb spiritual training from Chaplains Darrick Gutting, Rob Ginsburg, and David Thompson. They consistently spoke the Word of God to me and walked me through tough circumstances. I thank them for their service to me and my comrades.

I dedicate this book to my sister, Kristen. She is my Irish Twin, lifelong playmate, spiritual battle buddy, fellow therapist, a source of great laughter and joy, the craziest plant lady with the greenest thumb and the best eyelashes. Her Christ-like love for the lost and the least of this world motivates me. Kristen's reliance upon God to make beauty from ashes inspires me to commit to God's Kingdom purpose no matter what the world throws at me.

My husband, Barry, knew I couldn't hold his hand at church because I was busy writing sermon notes. I'm thankful for his input, support, and love — and not just for this project, but for all the home, family, military, and professional projects over the past 25 years. Sharing life with him has shaped me in countless ways.

Many blessings,
Katie

A Note from Pastor Chris

Sixteen years as a pastor and no one has ever wanted to write a book about my sermons. When Katie approached me about writing such a book, I was intrigued. I agreed to participate, and we met several times over the course of seven months. You will read about our book meetings.

As the Student and Family Pastor at CrossBridge Community Church in San Antonio, I shepherd a large flock of always changing and sometimes wandering sheep. On a typical Wednesday youth group night, I balance between my desire for revival in the flock and my reality check to just return all 150 sheep safely to their parents!

My work in ministry is a balancing act of preaching, teaching, counseling, corralling, correcting, and mentoring students. Oh, and staff meetings. I pray through it all. This book slowed me down as I considered the mysterious question: *What really happens with my sermons?* I suppose every pastor wonders, all the while trusting the Good Shepherd to do the heart-changing work.

Although I have seen ministry fruit over the years, I never gave prolonged thought to exploring the transformation that occurs after a *single* sermon in a *single* listening sheep. For one thing, I stay busy preparing the next sermon, and for another, it seems awkward to ask people specifics about how the weekly sermon changed them. The Word of God is active and does not return void. This book expresses the invisible, spiritual alteration following a sermon.

I am honored to be the pastor behind the sermons in this book. May you be doubly blessed by this work, first by the truth in the sermon messages and second by the expressions of Katie's spiritual growth from them.

To God be the glory,
Pastor Chris Dillashaw

A User's Guide to this Book

- Each chapter ends with sacred scripture and a song.
- The Word of God is spiritual nutrition.
- Take it in. Reflect. Meditate. Get strong by its power.
- We left a few conversation starters after each chapter to help get the mental wheels turning.

Reflections & A Tune
All Scripture is given by inspiration of God, and is profitable for doctrine, for reproof, for correction, for instruction in righteousness, that the man of God may be complete, thoroughly equipped for every good work. (2 Timothy 3:16-17)
Blessed are those who hunger and thirst for righteousness, For they shall be filled. (Matthew 5:6)
Take heed to yourself and to the doctrine. Continue in them, for in doing this you will save both yourself and those who hear you. (1 Timothy 4:16)
Give us this day our daily bread. (Matthew 6:11)
Song Recommendation: "Old Church Choir" by Zach Williams

A Book Club Guide

Grace and Mercy – A Devotional Journey is ideal for a book club. Gather your neighbors, friends, and co-workers and read this book together. Grow in your faith, week by week, chapter by chapter. This is a book with stories folded into stories. Book club members will be inspired to explore and share their own stories. When life is lived properly in community, its joys are multiplied and its sorrows are divided. Form a book club community and watch what unfolds.

Create a book club where you can gather with others, check your spiritual pulse, and examine the many expressions of grace and mercy in your life and the lives of those who show up to book club.

Sharing the sacredness of ordinary happenings in our lives honors God's life-giving Spirit. Take turns hosting book club in one another's homes or at your local church or community center. You may even find it helpful to take turns leading the week's discussion.

Use the conversation starters at the end of each chapter as group discussion questions. This book will stir your heart toward love and goodness and encourage the habit of meeting together to discuss your thoughts and feelings.

Specific Suggestions for a Successful Book Club

- An ideal book club has between 5 and 8 members. Members should have their own copy of the book.

- Assign one chapter of reading each week so members attend the group having already read the text, but feel free to re-read some of that week's chapter aloud to refresh the material. Give each member a chance to read aloud or to pose the discussion question. Pace yourself based on the group's size and speed of processing, but try to cover one chapter each week.

- Consider starting each book club meeting with a "round robin" time where you inquire about each member's insights and response to the chapter. Do this by inviting everyone to share his or her general reflections on the text before asking the specific questions.

- Feel free to ask your own questions of the group members. Encourage members to think of a discussion question for each week's gathering.

- Encourage members to come with their answers to the conversation starters written down in the book or in a separate journal.

- Know that everyone will have an answer, but not everyone will want to answer every question. Allow them to say, "pass" and move on to the next book club member for a response.

- People process differently. Accept and expect variation in responses. Variety is excellent! Create a culture of honor so that each member is respected for his or her contribution to the discussion.

- Snacks foster sharing! When people are snacking, they often feel comfortable which strengthens a willingness to be vulnerable and share more deeply. Ask book club members to take turns bringing a snack to share with the group. Food and fellowship go together. There are a few chapters that include references to certain foods; feel free to be intentional about including those foods during that week's book club meeting.

- Listen to the suggested song as a group. Read the lyrics. Ask for members' reactions to the song and how it applies to their lives.

- Study and explore the additional scriptures at the end of each chapter for a more Bible-study focused book club. Encourage members to memorize or meditate on one or more of the passages provided and then ask for their insights and reflections.

- The book is about the discipleship process between a pastor and a church member. Explore this concept with the members of your book club. Ask members what the recent sermon at their church was about and how it influenced their week's experience.

Prayer

Heavenly Father,

Grant wisdom to each reader's heart.

Heal them with Your Word and lead them in Your way.

Through the work of Your Holy Spirit, excite hearts, enlighten minds, and enrich lives.

In Jesus' name,

Amen

1 - Cold Front

"Robust grass endures mighty winds;
loyal ministers endure through ordeal."

Unknown

The mercury dropped drastically as a cold front moved across Texas. Outside, Live Oak trees whipped under the powerful wind. I hated to get out of bed, but the weight of the heavy blanket was not doing its calming work. My mind remained cluttered and clogged. Writing out my thoughts seemed the shortest route to clarity and eventual sleep. I knew this routine.

Writing is like cleaning out mental closets. I had been hoarding thoughts and stuffing feelings all week. Things were untidy. I reluctantly reminded myself that life is a process — an untidy process. A process through time. No one escapes the untidiness of life *or* the effects of time. Yet, I felt, once again, my attempt to escape both. Sleep is the honest barometer for my emotional state. My barometer was registering *fretfully awake*.

I faced the cold of the room. I dug through the clutter of my actual closet. I found my winter bathrobe — the black and red one I'd bought when we lived in Massachusetts during the worst winter they'd had in a decade. In the family room just outside the bedroom, I snuggled into the rocking chair Barry had bought me years ago when I was pregnant with Joshua. We lived in Colorado then. I thought about the fourteen different places I've called home over the years.

I opened my computer on my lap and began typing. I wrote about the things that shaped and molded my week, my mind like a movie reel on replay. I revisited what transpired; I reviewed my interactions with others. Random and racing thoughts came out as incomplete sentences. Put it all down as typed-out text was the first step. It was Friday. I was trying to remember what the pastor had preached on Sunday. I should have taken notes. I needed solid ground of truth right now. I promised myself to buy a notebook and always take it to church.

Maybe it was the cold front that was messing with my mind. I had a vague sense of being absent in my life and a disappointment to others. I felt behind schedule for things I wasn't even sure were *on* my schedule. I tried to write a to-do list to see if there was something I had forgotten to do. Oftentimes, free-association writing jogs my memory and reveals something I have forgotten to finish. I typed out my yet-undone tasks. There were several.

Suddenly, I remembered Sunday's sermon. Well, part of it. I remember the part about what Jesus said, "My Father has been working until now, and I have been working." (John 5:17). I prayed and asked God to reveal His work. More than anything else, I needed the reassurance that Jesus was at work in my life. I already knew that His Spirit lived in me. I got that truth down. Yielding to the Spirit was a different story. I stumbled in many ways. Words flowed through the small keyboard and onto the laptop screen. I typed something about the mysterious interplay between my choices and God's sovereignty. I wished I would have taken notes on Sunday. What else did the pastor say? I rocked in my rocking chair, purposefully slowing down my breathing. The wind whipped the trees outside. I heard the whistle through our chimney. I reached for an afghan and draped it over the back of my shoulders and around my neck.

Each sentence I typed lightened my internal stress load. Thoughts eventually unraveled and untangled themselves. My mental closet was getting organized, the slow way, just like a physical closet. I had cleaned out the front hallway closet last month. Where had all the stuff come from? Outgrown articles of clothing, random remnants from days-gone-by, Josh's tennis shoes, Barry's camouflage hunting gloves, William's paintball marker, the cheap raincoat I forgot I paid too much for when it rained at the concert in Virginia, the wrapping paper I bought on sale after Christmas last year, all crowded together in disarray.

I continued rocking in my chair and considered the untidiness of my crowded mental closet. I handled each thought, considered its origin and future: Does it stay? Give it away? Throw it out? Some thoughts needed to be thrown out for there was no value in them. The emotions attached to each thought got attention, too. Why did thinking *that* make me feel *that*? I kept digging and sorting. Most of what I discovered needed tossing. I was stripping things down to bare essentials.

My mental closet turned into a visual image of a bus. Each thought and each feeling was a passenger — some harmless, some not so much, some invited, some stowaways. One by one, I was stopping the bus and letting each off. I pictured a funny scene where the demanding feeling of anger tried to take over and drive the bus. My Army buddy Alan once shared his Georgia backwoods approach to spiritual warfare. He said, "Never let the devil ride; 'fore long, that fool wanna drive." I imagined Mr. Stowaway Anger trying to drive and wreck my bus! I prayed again, asking Jesus to be at work in my mind and for the strength to take every thought captive to be obedient to Him.

I thought and typed a lot about other people. I thought about our family's church friends, William's school friends, and Joshua's Navy buddies. I thought about my parents and my three sisters and their collective sixteen children. That took a while. I also thought about my two sisters-in-law and their four children and two grandchildren. My father-in-law, Poppie Bob, has a fairly new diagnosis of Alzheimer's. I cried as I considered his decline. More thoughts. More time. The process was one of emotional house cleaning. There was a prayer inside each thought. I shared every burden with God who graciously brought comfort. I considered Psalm 94's rhetorical questions, "He who planted the ear, shall He not hear? He who formed the eye, shall He not see?" (v. 9). My soul knew that God was right there with me in the middle of my late-night musings.

Sleep still seemed far off, so I put my laptop on the coffee table and walked to the end of the hall to my office. I searched the bookshelves for something to read. With hundreds of books to choose from, each one special in some way, I couldn't find the right one. I wanted something genuine and easy to read, something with solid truth, which my heart desperately needed. None jumped off the shelf. I flipped through the picture Bible that had been the boys' when they were young. I saw the cartoon from the book of Esther about the king not being able to sleep. The sleepless king had people bring books and read to him. The ancient truth that there's nothing new under the sun, including books as the antidote to insomnia, made me smile.

I left my office and sat on the staircase landing next to a decorative storage box. It was the first time I ever sat there. I opened the box and started looking through it. It's full of old cards and letters. I found a letter on pink stationery. It was dated 1993, and came from Kristi. She was writing to tell me that she would be my college roommate. She's my best friend to this day.

I found a card from my friend Kathryn who lives in Kentucky. She mailed it to me when I was deployed with the Army to Afghanistan. She had copied Isaiah 46:9-10 inside: "For I am God, and there is no other; I am God, and there is none like Me, Declaring the end from the beginning, And from ancient times things that are not yet done, Saying, 'My counsel shall stand, And I will do all My pleasure.' Calling a bird of prey from the east, the man who executes My counsel, from a far country. Indeed I have spoken it; I will also bring it to pass. I have purposed it; I will also do it."

This was just what I needed. I sat for several minutes on that carpeted stair, a spot well-worn from my dog who normally nestles there when the sunshine streams in from the large window. I could see his black hair collected on the beige carpet of the stairs' crevice. The messiness of it bothered me. Vacuuming was out of the question because Barry and William were fast asleep. Besides, I prefer the quieter chore of ironing. I ran my fingers along the crease and collected a generous pinch of dog hair.

I took Kathryn's card and the dog hair downstairs. I threw the hair in the kitchen's garbage and returned to my rocking chair. I re-read the card. Its truth drew me in. I picked up my laptop and typed the verse, personalizing it in my own interpretation: *God is God. The only one. What He wants to do, He will do. This cold front is His work. He makes the wind blow. The howling wind shows His invisible power. God is always at work. Even this sleepless night is His. God's purposes will stand.*

I sat there rocking for a long time. For years I've pictured the tension in me like a kangaroo who demands movement. Running in the day and rocking at night helps ease that tension. I listened to the strong winds through our chimney. I experienced a deep stillness. The peace of a cleaned-out emotional closet surrounded me. The mental clutter was gone. The clogged brain pipes were clear. Jesus was driving my bus; my good thoughts and honest feelings were obediently sitting in their bus seats as contented passengers. I felt sleepy.

Careful to not wake Barry, I snuck into our bedroom, flung my bathrobe on the floor, and crawled under the heavy blanket. The furnace kicked on and startled the dog who was asleep in the corner of the room. I heard him shift positions. If I got up to open the bedroom door, he would likely move to his spot on the stairs. I wanted to get up and go back to my laptop to add something about how the unpredictable changes in weather match the changes in my thoughts and feelings. I decided to lie still, keep the door closed, and write about the weather tomorrow. As I drifted off, I prayed. I asked God to use this sleepless night as He had used King Xerxes' so long ago. I told

Him I wanted courage like Esther, that I too was ready for such a time as this. I wanted to see His work unfold in a kingdom purpose for my life. I curled up and slept soundly.

Reflections & A Tune

That night the king could not sleep. So one was commanded to bring the book of the records of the chronicles; and they were read before the king. (Esther 6:1)

For the weapons of our warfare are not carnal but mighty in God for pulling down strongholds, casting down arguments and every high thing that exalts itself against the knowledge of God, bringing every thought into captivity to the obedience of Christ, and being ready to punish all disobedience when your obedience is fulfilled. (2 Corinthians 10:4-6)

He gives snow like wool.
He scatters the frost like ashes;
He casts out His hail like morsels;
Who can stand before His cold?
He sends out His word and melts them;
He causes His wind to blow, and the waters flow.
(Psalm 147:16-18)

Song Recommendation: "Hold Me Jesus" by Rich Mullins

Conversation Starters

- How do you keep track of what your pastor teaches?
- Do you ever go back and review your sermon notes?
- How does a jam-packed week affect your sleep?
- What do you do when you can't sleep?
- Have you recognized God's purpose for your life? Do tell!

2 - Walgreens

"A person often meets his destiny on
the road he took to avoid it."
Jean de La Fontaine

On a Sunday morning in February 2019, Pastor Chris Dillashaw preached about the iconic Valentine's Day conversation candy hearts. Instantly, I knew I would write about Chris and his sermons. It was like I saw a future book of them. The force of the feeling was strong, but I dismissed it entirely. I silently expressed resistance and mentally listed my excuses of ineligibility to writing a book.

Then, months later, on a Wednesday night (April 3, 2019) when Pastor Chris taught Romans 9, the pressured feeling of the book came a second time. My heart raced in rebellion against the thought. I couldn't write a book about Pastor Chris's sermons. It seemed impossible. I write diaries not books. I write at night when I can't sleep. I write silly poems and kids' stories that stay hidden in my office. I read books — not *write* them.

During my professional career, I wrote and published a workbook with a colleague, and I wrote science articles and book chapters, but writing a *real* book for *real* readers to be sold in a *real* bookstore, that was not something I could do. Besides, I would have to approach Chris and share the idea and risk his suspicion and rejection. My internal resistance was not something I could overcome. And yet, the thoughts of the book needled my mind all day.

The very next morning, I went out and about to run errands. Walgreens should have been my *last* stop. It's closest to my home and on the same side of the street, but for some reason I went there first. Walking around Walgreens, I internally criticized myself. Now I would have to cross traffic and zigzag around to get back on the highway. My mental war was interrupted when I realized that the person in the cashier's line in front of me was Pastor Chris. For the six years I've lived in San Antonio, I've never seen Chris in Walgreens. (I haven't seen him there since.)

The Lord directs our steps. When I saw Chris, I felt that God was underlining and italicizing the whisper, w*rite the book*. I said hello to Chris. He had been next door at a barbeque restaurant at a meeting with his boss, our church's lead pastor. I told Chris how affected I was from his sermon the night before. Chris said, "Well, Bless God." I did not say a word about the possibility of the book.

My heart rate climbed. I introduced Chris to Rodney, the check-out guy, who had become a friend over the past years. Their small talk was a welcomed distraction.

The next day, Chris's wife, Ann Marie, texted me, "How are you doing? Checking on you" (with Emojis!). After a few exchanges, my heart overflowed through my texting thumbs. I told Ann Marie that I saw her hubby in Walgreens and that I wanted to write a book about Chris's sermons. She wrote me back that Chris would love it. Wives. We know things. With Ann Marie's confidence in Chris's interest, I emailed Chris and got on his calendar for today, May 9, 2019. I am typing this a few hours after our first book meeting.

Reflections & A Tune

A man's heart plans his way, but the LORD directs his steps. (Proverbs 16:9)

Oh LORD, how great are Your works!
Your thoughts are very deep. (Psalm 92:5)

And He is before all things, and in Him all things consist. (Colossians 1:17)

So, affectionately longing for you, we were well pleased to impart to you not only the gospel of God, but also our own lives, because you had become dear to us. (1 Thess. 2:8)

Song Recommendation: "Directions" by Micah Tyler

Conversation Starters

- Have you ever been afraid to tell someone your dream?

- Do you ever do things out of a logical order and then immediately see a God-ordained reason for your being where you ended up?

- If you could do something you love and know you wouldn't fail, what would you do? (Thanks for sharing. Now go and do it!)

- When you're afraid of what's coming next, how do you pray? Give an example of this in your life.

- Tell of a meeting you had that changed your destiny.

3 - Seashells

Book Meeting, May 9

"It takes a lot courage to show your dreams to someone else."
Erma Bombeck

We met in Pastor Chris's office at the church. It's a simple office: small, sparsely furnished, yet busy with remnants of all kinds — mementos from sermons gone by stacked on top of his desk, pinned on bulletin boards, hanging on the walls, lying on his book shelf. I like to glance around this office. When I see these remnant objects, I remember the sermons. To me they're spiritual seashells.

As a young girl, long before I'd dared to dream that I could see the ocean, I understood why people who *had been* to the ocean collected seashells. A seashell is an instant reminder of the living, churning ocean. In the 1970s, seashells were a staple of bathroom décor. I used to hold the seashells in my Mom and Dad's peach-colored bathroom. I held the biggest conch shell to my ear, convinced I could hear crashing waves and be transported to the salty seaside where I hoped one day to dip my toes.

Chris's office is chock-full of spiritual seashells. Coming out of my little trance, I blurted, "Chris, let me write up my notes from your sermons. Each sermon will be a chapter."

I was too shy to mention seashells.

I continued, "Ten, maybe twenty, chapters. A book about you, a pastor, and me, one of your sheep, and how we follow Jesus. Do you ever wonder what us sheep hear and think when you preach?"

I drifted away in thought about pastors, all pastors everywhere, especially shepherding pastors. How can pastors *ever* know how their sermons affect us? Don't they wonder how their words influence the sheep? There are so many sheep, each with a unique way to see and receive. I thought about Paul's first letter to the Corinthians where he tells them how it pleased God by the foolishness of preaching to save those who believe. God clearly intended for preaching. I like this idea of job security for pastors. I also like seashells to point us toward the sea and preaching to point us to Christ. I like that, too.

My brain can't recall what more was said today — our first book meeting in May. I just know this: Chris agreed to participate. I was happy. The cloud of anticipated rejection, which had followed me into the meeting, evaporated. I was going to write a book, a devotional book of sorts, about what happens with the sermons, both Sunday and Wednesday sermons.

Chris prayed. He instinctively does. I also prayed. I started praying *out loud* ten years back when I was stationed in Natick, Massachusetts with the Army. My family attended a tiny church less than a mile from our tiny rental house. With so few of us in church each week, I never knew when the pastor would ask me to open up the dialogue with God. *Out loud*. Praying is like breathing. The Scripture says, "pray without ceasing." Breath without ceasing maintains physical life. Prayer without ceasing maintains spiritual life. Praying, like breathing is life-giving. But praying out loud is like trying to breathe naturally when everyone is listening to your breath. Ten years ago, I learned this: focus on God who *gives* us breath, and the breath takes care of itself. Prayer is the same. With God now dwelling within us we are only a breath away from being in touch with His divine presence. And when words won't come, just keep breathing and trusting and focusing on God who gives and sustains life.

Romans 8:26-27 is our prayer safety net:

> For we do not know what we should pray for as we ought, but the Spirit Himself makes intercession for us with groanings which cannot be uttered. Now He who searches the hearts knows what the mind of the Spirit is, because He makes intercession for the saints according to the will of God.

In prayer, Chris and I praised God for His goodness and His grace. And now here *you* are holding the book. Our request is simple: learn and share. After twenty years of saturation in Army culture, I work from the KISS principle: Keep It Simple, Soldier.

Perhaps Jesus, our Good Shepherd, was inviting us to simplicity when he said:

> Therefore I say to you, do not worry about your life, what you will eat, or what you will drink; nor about your body, what you will put on. Is not life more than food, and the body more than clothing? Look at the birds of the air: for they neither sow

nor reap nor gather into barns; yet your heavenly Father feeds them. Are you not of more value than they?

(Matthew 6:25-26).

When the Apostle Paul wrote his second letter to Timothy, he told him be diligent and come to see him and he told him to bring his coat and his books and the parchments (2 Timothy 4:9;13). I always smile when I read that in Paul's letter because I hope to live that simply when I am old. I just need a friend who will visit and bring me books and things to write on!

Reflections & A Tune
Bless the LORD, O my soul! O LORD my God, You are very great; You are clothed with honor and majesty, who covers Yourself with light as with a garment, Who stretch out the heavens like a curtain. (Psalm 104:1-2)
And whatever you do in word or deed, do all in the name of the Lord Jesus, giving thanks to God the Father through Him. (Colossians 3:17)
The eyes of the LORD are on the righteous and his ears are attentive to their cry. (Psalm 34:15)
Song Recommendation: "My Story" by Big Daddy Weave

Conversation Starters

- What spiritual seashells do you carry in your memory bank?

- Who has the coolest office you've ever sat in and looked around at their collection of trinkets? What is on display in your office and why do you have those items?

- How often do you pray out loud for others? What has been your experience?

- In what ways are you trying to simplify your life?

4 - Sweet Candy!

"In prayer it is better to have a heart
without words than words without a heart."

John Bunyan

Sunday February 17, 2019, was the last day of Discipleship-Now. *D-Now* is an annual, three-day youth revival at CrossBridge Community Church in San Antonio led by Chris, the Pastor of Students and Families. I am one of twenty-five adults who volunteer to serve with Chris's ministry, which is called "Ablaze." Chris has been the Youth Pastor since 2005. This is my second year as one of his volunteer Life Group Leaders. I had thirteen 14-year old girls (and Leah, a college student assigned as my helper) at my house since Friday night. The D-Now weekend was packed with worship, sermons, life group sessions, Bible studies, an in-town community-outreach, late-night talking, and plenty of praying. And so there we were in church on Sunday morning, waiting for Pastor Chris's final D-Now sermon. His fourth message in three days! How many caffeinated drinks were necessary to keep Chris at peak preaching performance? Only Ann Marie knows! Almost two-hundred sleep-deprived students from thirty area schools, plus college student volunteers and Life Group Leaders packed into the seats, all wearing matching yellow D-Now T-shirts.

I was still digesting the spiritual nutrition of the Saturday night message Chris had given less than fifteen hours earlier. That sermon stirred the hearts of eleven young teenagers to turn in faith, accept the free gift of God's grace, and believe on the Lord Jesus Christ. That meant eleven new children in God's family!

I tried to pray as Chris walked to the stage, but my tired mind raced to later that afternoon which was the day selected to celebrate my younger son William's 17th birthday. How was I going to clean up the house, grocery shop for the week, and squeeze in a nap before William's friends showed up? But, as Chris started preaching, the Holy Spirit ministered peace to me. My worries evaporated. I started to take notes. Immediately upon gaining focus and energy, the vision of this book flashed as an awareness in my inner being. I knew God's plan for me to write it. The plan was a clear and sudden vision. I wish I had responded with joy, excitement, and acceptance. Not so! Now, almost one hundred days later, I am using those sermon notes to write this chapter.

Chris pulled out a gigantic, heart-shaped box of chocolates, which he admitted he buys each year on February 15th because of the 75% price reduction. He also pulled out a small box of candy conversation hearts. He is the only one in his family who likes the chalk-tasting, heart-shaped candy so he doesn't have to hide his stash of them.

Chris recounted his childhood years growing up in church. When the church doors were opened, he and his family were there. Chris believed and trusted in Jesus Christ at age eight. Years later though, as a young college freshman at Baylor University, he found himself perplexed by the dual nature of his life. On the one hand, he had Christian friends and did Christian-like things with them. On the other hand, he had non-Christian friends and acted in un-Christian ways when with them. Chris was struggling with the tension in what he termed his "covert Christian life." He felt unsettled in his spiritual being and had been praying that God would reveal Himself. One evening, as the battle arose in Chris' heart, he walked to the top of a five-story campus parking garage. He was wrestling with God and felt like his striving was never-ending and never good enough. Chris remembers the feeling of having an intimate exchange with God he styled as "loving but severe." He called it a "pull-up-a-chair-and-sit-knee-to-knee" conversation with God. Through His Holy Spirit, God revealed His love to Chris: a love that is free with no strings attached. There is no need for performing or for apologies for past misgivings. It is not a matter of striving. You don't need to wander around in the wilderness of shame and self-doubt. God called Chris to a surrendered life in the reality of His abundant, free-of-charge and free-for-the-taking, *unconditional* love.

The Scripture that Chris anchors to that day's transformational conversation with God says,

> Oh the depth of the riches both of the wisdom and knowledge of God! How unsearchable are His judgments and His ways past finding out! For who has known the mind of the LORD? Or who has become His counselor? Or who has first given to Him and it shall be repaid to him? For of Him and through Him and to Him are all things, to whom be glory forever. Amen. (Romans 11:33-36).

Chris broke this Scripture down, imagining it as if it were printed on candy conversation hearts.

God Is Rich

Oh the depth of the riches of God! Psalm 50:10:12 tells us what God declares through the writing of Asaph, a Hebrew poet, song-writer, and worship leader.

> For every beast of the forest is Mine,
> And the cattle on a thousand hills.
> I know all the birds of the mountains.
> And the wild beast of the field are Mine.
> If I were hungry, I would not tell you;
> For the world is Mine, and all its fullness.

We do well to remember that anything we have is on loan to us from the LORD. It's all His. We are but humble borrowers.

God Is Smart

Human beings can acquire knowledge. We can gain understanding. We can grow in wisdom. But our knowledge, understanding, and wisdom are incomplete and have a fading quality. We forget things. We wander away from truths. And, the more we learn, the more we forget. Not only are we limited in capacity, we are prone to settle for the wisdom of this world rather than endeavor toward God's wisdom. In 1 Corinthians 3:19, Paul writes, "For the wisdom of this world is foolishness with God." And then Paul immediately quotes from the Old Testament books of Job and Psalms and writes, "For it is written, "He catches the wise in their own craftiness," and again, "The LORD knows the thoughts of the wise, that they are futile."

In contrast, God's wisdom and knowledge are complete, never wandering, never fading. There is nothing that God can learn. He is called The Ancient of Days. God already knows exactly what He has always known, which is everything, including the parts of life we consider in the future. (God is outside the boundaries of time). The only thing God forgets is what He says He will forget. In Isaiah 43:25 we read, "I, even I, am He who blots out your transgressions for My own sake; And I will not remember your sins." The promise of God to willfully forget our sins is seen in Jeremiah 31:34 and repeated in Hebrews 10:17.

Even His forgetting is done with perfect intention. Isaiah 40:28 says, "Have you not known? Have you not heard? The everlasting God, the LORD, the Creator of the ends of the earth, neither faints nor is weary. His understanding is unsearchable."

Can't Judge God

Job questioned God. We do too. I have put God's ways on the examination table of my mind and tuned up the magnification of my analytical microscope. Scrutinizing. Searching. Judging.

In the middle of a trial or tragedy we ask God to account for our unfortunate circumstances. We ask "Why, God?" Job had four friends visit him during his season of grief. Mostly their advice was wrong and God corrects them, but Job's friend Zophar rightly asked Job, "Can you search out the deep things of God? Can you find out the limits of the Almighty?" (Job 11:7). In the end, we see God respond to Job with seventy-seven questions of His own. Talk about a pull-up-a-chair-and-sit-knee-to-knee" conversation! "Then the LORD answered Job out of the whirlwind, and said, "Who is this who darkens counsel by words without knowledge? Now prepare yourself like a man; I will question you, and you shall answer Me." (Job 38:1-3). Isaiah 55:8-9 helps us know why we need not ask the question "why?" "For My thoughts are not your thoughts; nor are your ways My ways," says the LORD. "For as the heavens are higher than the earth, so are My ways higher than your ways, And My thoughts than your thoughts."

God Is Perfect

God is without error. He is *perfectly* perfect. Our finite minds simply cannot comprehend God's perfection. Deuteronomy 32:4 says, "Ascribe greatness to our God. He is the Rock, His work is perfect; For all His ways are justice, A God of truth and without injustice; righteous and upright is He." Having a right view of God's perfection shifts me into submissive obedience. When I realize the truth of 2 Corinthians 5:21, I am humbled into stillness, awe, and gratitude. It reads, "For He made Him who knew no sin to be sin for us, that we might become the righteousness of God in Him." When Chris spoke of God's perfection, I was reminded to maintain a healthy view of other human beings. I unwisely put people on pedestals, expecting perfection. I also do that to myself. As Chris talked about his conversation with God on the top of the parking garage at Baylor University, I was encouraged to keep *only* God on the throne where only *He* is eligible to sit in perfection.

Unstoppable

Chris took us back to 1986 and his fifth-grade year by recounting his elementary school crush on a young girl named Colleen. She was a strong athlete who was brave enough to play soccer at recess with the boys. Chris liked that! He was impressed. He thought she was the best. He thought she was unstoppable. He gave her a Valentine! We all relate to ascribing godlike qualities to people other than God, and it does seem to start in elementary school! In truth, only God is unstoppable. We return to Job to hear how he spoke rightly of God after his encounter with Him.

> Then Job answered the LORD and said: "I know that You can do everything, And that no purpose of Yours can be withheld from You. (Job 42:2).

We hear from God in Isaiah 46:9-10, "Remember the former things of old, For I am God, and there is no other; I am God, and there is none like Me. Declaring the end from the beginning, and from ancient times things that are not yet done, saying, "My counsel shall stand, and I will do all My pleasure."

Chris closed his sermon with a history lesson on those tiny, colorful, chalky conversation hearts. They were invented by Oliver Chase during the Civil War. They were originally wafers, shaped as hearts with customized messages written in icing and sent to soldiers fighting in the war. God's conversation with us is a lot like those original conversation heart wafers. We are soldiers in the Lord's Army, fighting in a spiritual battle for truth. And as we put on the full armor of God and take our stand against our adversary who seeks our destruction, may we remember to converse daily with God through His word. Write it across your heart that God IS rich. God IS smart. God IS perfect. God IS unstoppable. And may the fact that we cannot judge God be a source of peace and not confusion. Truth like that brings a peace that passes all understanding, and let's call that peace: "freedom."

Reflections & A Tune
I have treasured the words of His mouth more than my necessary food. (Job 23:12b)
...he who is of a merry heart has a continual feast. (Proverbs 15:15b)
Now He who searches the hearts knows what the mind of the Spirit is, because He makes intercession for the saints according to the will of God. (Romans 8:27)
And you will see Me and find Me, when you search for Me with all your heart. (Jeremiah 29:13)
Song Recommendation: "Stand in Your Love" by Josh Baldwin

Conversation Starters

- Have you ever had a pull-up-a-chair-and-sit-knee-to-knee conversation with God? If so, what was it like? And, what was it about?

- What is your biggest barrier of acceptance to God's love for you?

- How would your life change if you thought deeply and more often of God's perfection in all His attributes?

- How can a decision to stop judging God be a source of peace of mind?

5 - Food For Thought

Book Meeting, May 30

> "Popcorn for breakfast! Why not? It's a grain.
> It's like, like, grits, but with high self-esteem."
>
> James Patterson

At the end of one of Chris's sermons, he pulled out hundreds of Little Debbie Star Crunch Crisp snacks. He'd brought them to share with the teens attending Ablaze. The link between the Star Crunch Crisp snacks and his message was something about there never being enough of those delicious, chocolate-covered, crunchy rice cakes to satisfy our hunger, but *God* is enough to satisfy our deepest hunger: *spiritual* hunger. And, God is always enough. I remember scribbling a little list as Chris talked. "God is big enough, strong enough, faithful enough, kind enough, and forgiving enough." At the bottom of my little list, I wrote in big letters, "God *is* enough." And, then I wrote and circled, "He satisfies."

Chris was smart to teach those teens about hunger. Many of them are spiritually anorexic, or even bulimic. Either they didn't take in enough of the Word of God or took it in and then tossed it up too soon, before the benefits of nutrition could take hold. Both spiritual anorexia and bulimia deny the teen's spiritual development. Why do I say *teen* here? I should not single them out as a safe people group to epitomize a universal need. I am a mother of two sons, one of them still a teenager, and *just* as hungry and *just* as prone to starve or binge.

I was thinking about the Star Crunch Crisps as I walked into Chris's office for our book meeting today. The memory of his Little Debbie message was active in my hungry soul. I said something like, "Chris, you're like the spiritual chef at a restaurant, and I am, and others are, like patrons of the restaurant. You make the spiritual meal. We partake." I forgot to say the follow-through part about us receiving nutrition and the health and strength that follows so we can convert spiritual energy into physical drive to spread the message of God's love and hope. I am sure he got the gist of my thoughts.

Chris smiled but immediately adjusted my comparison. He told me that Dave Buzby, his old mentor, gave him that same analogy long ago, but correctly labeled the pastor as the waiter, for it can only be the Holy Spirit who serves as chef. And, week after week, sermon after sermon, there's only one item on the menu: Jesus, the Living Water and the Bread of Life.

I told Chris how adding Wednesday nights (Ablaze) to my life healed my spiritual anorexia. I told him that I am now well-fed and up to my fighting weight, ready to train; ready to fight for truth in the spiritual realm; ready to be of use in God's kingdom. I forgot to thank him for being the Ablaze waiter, faithfully serving the message of Jesus as the main entrée every week.

Chris talked deeper into the food-for-thought analogy. He does that. His brain fiddles with comparisons like a master locksmith with a safe. I figured that out a long while back. He said that he is the waiter and is happy to serve, but each person must show up hungry. And not just show up hungry, but be aware of their hunger and willing to digest his/her own (spiritual) meal.

After our book meeting, I thought a lot about the morsels of truth on my drive to the grocery store. I turned the radio off. Having the radio on when my mind is full is like pouring water into a potted plant when the soil is already drenched. Time must pass. Thoughts must be absorbed. Chris must have meant something like this when he talked about digesting sermons.

Digestion of truth is like a plant: sitting, soaking, and waiting so that every cell is changed, energized, strengthened, and transformed into new growth. I thought about the varieties of fruit and flowers and herbs and spices that grow on well-nourished plants and trees, all because the soil uses the nutrition provided.

I kept my radio off many miles. What popped into my mind on the ride home from the grocery store was Psalm 34:8, "Oh, taste and see that the Lord is good; blessed is the man who trusts in Him." I couldn't remember that it was Psalm 34, but when I got home, I looked it up. I guess Dave Busby wasn't the first man named David to compare physical hunger to spiritual hunger.

Reflections & A Tune
Then they said to Him, "Lord, give us this bread always." And Jesus said to them, "I am the bread of life. He who comes to Me shall never hunger, and he who believes in Me shall never thirst. (John 6:34-35)
Therefore, laying aside all malice, all deceit, hypocrisy, envy, and all evil speaking, as newborn babes, desire the pure milk of the word, that you may grow thereby if indeed you have tasted that the Lord is gracious. (1 Peter 2:1-3)
But you are those who have continued with Me in My trials. And I bestow upon you a kingdom, just as My Father bestowed one upon Me, that you may eat and drink at My table in My kingdom, and sit on thrones judging the twelve tribes of Israel. (Luke 22:28-30)
For though by this time you ought to be teachers, you need someone to teach you again the first principles of the oracles of God; and you have come to need milk and not solid food. For everyone who partakes only of milk is unskilled in the word of righteousness, for he is a babe. But solid food belongs to those who are of full age, that is, those who by reason of use have their senses exercised to discern both good and evil. (Hebrews 5:12)
Song Recommendation: "Come to the Table" by Sidewalk Prophets

Conversation Starters

- Describe a time or a season when you felt spiritually bulimic or anorexic. What helped you turn things around?
- Can you think of your pastor as the waiter serving up a Holy Spirit-prepared meal for you on a Sunday or a Wednesday?
- Is there anything that you do to help "digest" the sermons you hear each week?
- Would you be willing to keep silent in your car as a way to process your thoughts and to contemplate things at a deeper level?

6 - Clean Up on Aisle Two!

> "A man who desires revenge should dig two graves."
>
> Unknown

I hope that what happened to me in December 2018 happens to you. I went to church on a Sunday morning with an unresolved emotional issue pressing down on my chest like an elephant. (Think: in-law issue exacerbated by the holidays). And when Chris stood up to preach, he addressed my issue with crystal clarity and laser focus. I was like, *WHAT?*

The feeling of being preached to directly is unique. My first thought was that Chris stole my diary and read all the entries marked BEWARE. DARK THOUGHTS. Thankfully, I snapped out of my emotional flashback when I remembered that I haven't kept a diary since the 8th grade. (I grew up with three sisters, so keeping a diary was risky business).

Chris prayed. He starts his sermons by recognizing the joy of coming together as a faith family and then prays for the Holy Spirit to lead and guide his message. He humbly asks for prayer for himself, which is great because now I automatically start praying for him when I see him walk toward the stage.

Chris read Psalm 27. Here's some of it:

> The LORD is my light and my salvation;
> Whom shall I fear?
> The LORD is the strength of my life;
> Of Whom shall I be afraid?
> When the wicked came against me
> To eat up my flesh,
> My enemies and foes,
> They stumbled and fell.
> Though an army may encamp against me,
> My heart shall not fear;
> Though war may rise against me,
> In this I will be confident.

My mind and heart traveled back in time to when I was deployed to Afghanistan. Psalm 27 is a "Bunker Psalm," at least in my mind. Chris told us to hold this Psalm's message in our minds as he read chapter 24 of First Samuel, which is a dicey little story of a real-life conflict between two mighty men: Saul and David. Saul was the King of Israel and David was his known successor, anointed by God through Samuel. The tension between these two men was real and rising. Saul, and three thousand of his *special operations* military men were chasing David to kill him. Saul went into a cave to use the bathroom. Guess who was hiding in the cave? That's right! David and his men. David's men encouraged David to strike Saul down, but instead David snuck up on Saul and merely cut off the hem of his robe. Moments later, outside the cave, David hollered after Saul to show him that he could have, but didn't, fatally harm him when he was in a vulnerable, unsuspecting position in the cave.

I like how it reads in The Living Bible, which tells that David says, "The Lord will decide between us. Perhaps he will kill you for what you are trying to do to me, but I will never harm you. As the old proverb says, 'Wicked is as wicked does,' but despite your wickedness, I'll not touch you. And who is the king of Israel trying to catch, anyway? Should he spend his time chasing one who is as worthless as a dead dog or flea? May the Lord judge as to which of us is right and punish whichever one of us is guilty. He is my lawyer and defender, and he will rescue me from your power!"

Notice the humble character of David: humility to remain under God's authority and to restrain every ounce of desire to slice Saul to bits when he had the chance. David had a distinct upper hand. Chris said that we may have a difficult person in our life. (Um, YEAH! Read my imaginary diary, Christopher!). God teaches us in the way He taught David thousands of years ago, that is *through* our difficult person. Chris emphasized the truth of David's declaration that God is our defender. God is our rescuer. As Psalm 27 says, we are confident in God, despite the conflict that rages. Chris asked us to surrender our pride and desire for vengeance to God's power that is ALL-mighty and ALL-powerful. In other words, humbly get out of God's way, and let Him work the miracle.

I imagined a dialogue:

Me: (prideful, childish, and self-willed): "I can handle my conflict. I have a few payback strategies concocted with more up my sleeve. I have plenty of dark thoughts about the one who hurt me!"

God: (gentle, wise, and patient): "Your strategies will never work. Trust me. I see the end from the beginning. My view is panoramic. Let me know when you want my help. I am right here, patiently waiting for you to reach the end of yourself. I have all the time in the world."

And now, back to *The Living Bible* for the miraculous change in Saul's perspective.

> Saul called back, "Is it really you, my son David?" Then he began to cry. And he said to David, "You are a better man than I am, for you have repaid me good for evil. Yes, you have been wonderfully kind to me today, for when the Lord delivered me into your hand, you didn't kill me. Who else in all the world would let his enemy get away when he had him in his power? May the Lord reward you well for the kindness you have shown me today. And now I realize that you are surely going to be king, and Israel shall be yours to rule. Oh, swear to me by the Lord that when that happens you will not kill my family and destroy my line of descendants!

Chris reiterated his message that God is a miracle-working God who is working *through* our difficult relationships. God arranges circumstances for our testing and training. Not a single molecule in the universe is outside the sovereign control of God. Our best response to a difficult person in our life is faith and humility. Faith grows by knowing and trusting God's strength. Humility comes by knowing and admitting our weakness. Our attempt to posture in self-defense, manipulate, get angry, control, and be spiteful is the most costly and the least effective method of dealing with a difficult person. Chris said, "Taking matters into your own hands is a lot like using the cheap, thin paper towels to clean up a heavy-duty mess. Your hands get dirty and you just smear the dirt around. Nothing really gets resolved. Metaphorically, we need God's Brawney-like paper towel power to do the job!"

Only God can change a person's heart and just as the 24th chapter of First Samuel demonstrates, the aggressive enemy is changed by love, not violent retaliation. Don't use the utterly ineffective method of cleaning up relationship issues with anger and aggression. It is emotionally expensive. It will cost you your peace. God's love is real, miraculous, healing, effective, and so cost-effective that it's free! God's free gift to us is Jesus, and when Jesus' power and wisdom are released, two lives changed: ours and our enemy's.

Four months after Chris's paper towel message, I was in his office picking out decorations for an upcoming Youth Ministry event, and I noticed an empty, tipped over cup and a small puddle of water on the floor. Someone in the earlier prayer meeting must have accidentally knocked over a drink and didn't notice it. I ran to the ladies' room and back, and as I was down on my hands and knees wiping up the spilled water with the handful of paper towels, the Holy Spirit whispered a reminder of Chris's December message of faith and humility in the face of a known enemy. Thanks be to God for His Brawney-strength, His ironclad defense of us, and His cleaning power! These days, I am taking all my messes to God!

Reflections & A Tune

Alexander the coppersmith did me much harm. *May the Lord repay* him according to his works. You must also beware of him, for he has greatly resisted our words. At my first defense no one stood with me but all forsook me. *May it not be charged against them.* But the Lord stood with me and strengthened me, so that the message might be preached fully through me, and that all the Gentiles might hear. Also I was delivered out of the mouth of the lion. And the Lord will deliver me from every evil work and preserve me for His heavenly kingdom. To Him be glory forever and ever. Amen! (2 Timothy 4:14-18, emphasis added)

...since indeed God considers it just to repay with affliction those who afflict you, and to grant relief to you who are afflicted as well as to us... (2 Thessalonians 1:6-7 ESV)

Beloved, do not avenge yourselves, but rather give place to wrath; for it is written, "Vengeance is Mine, I will repay," says the Lord. (Romans 12:19)

Song Recommendation: "Never Stop Fighting for Me" by Riley Clemmons

Conversation Starters

- Have you ever thought the pastor was preaching directly to you and your situation?

- How is God working through a difficult person in your life?

- What is your experience with anger and revenge?

- Has anything helped you forgive a hurtful person?

- How does knowing that God will act justly and right every wrong in your story affect you today?

7 -The Congo

> "I will go anywhere, provided it be forward."
> David Livingstone

I was double-booked this morning. This was not double-booked in time, but in two minds competing for attention. My former Army boss, Colonel Howard, used to tell me I had too many minds. It was his *Karate Kid* reference of Mr. Miagee's, a coded way to remind me to focus on one thing at a time.

One mind in my head was on the book meeting and my other mind on a business meeting. I was trying to concentrate, but I was dressed fancy for the business meeting that was downtown right after the book meeting. I felt awkward. Twenty years in combat boots and a uniform makes me uncomfortable in a fitted dress and high heels. Chris was in shorts and a t-shirt. He looked regular. I told him I was overdressed for our book meeting. He said it was fine. He knew about my business meeting. He asked about it straight away. I told him I was excited about possibly buying a franchise, but still searching for God's wisdom as to whether or not it was His will for me and my husband. My inner seventh- grade girl was focusing on my stupid dress. If my dad could have seen me, he would have good-humoredly called me "Dotty." That's what he calls my mom when she wears her polka-dotted dress.

Chris said he had read the latest portion of the book. He was asking "How can our book benefit the Body of Christ?" Before I could answer, I thought how great a question it was. One intriguing thing about words: they ask *and* answer. I sometimes loathe the answering part of me. It's too busy searching. It's the part with too many minds. I want to wake up the little girl in me. She has the questions. She also has the stories. Come to think of it, she loved wearing dresses.

I told Chris that our book could feature dual perspectives, intertwined or even blended. It was going to be a book about his spiritual seashells (I still needed to tell him about the seashells) and how I had collected them in my mind — how the seashells were cues to my heart to remember important things. We both were searching and asking, almost hoping to convince the other that the book structure was there, but knowing it wasn't *quite* there.

I thought out loud: "Maybe I should write about Andrew and Morgan and how they fit into the Ablaze Ministry. I could write up their teaching lessons, too. Make it a potpourri. Drew: so funny; and Morgan: so passionate. There's so much material for a book about Ablaze." Even as I spoke my thoughts, I was pretty sure that direction was farther away from the what God had planted in my heart for this book. The more I tried to get details by remembering my *I-must-write-a-book experience*, the more the details escaped me.

Chris suggested to wait and think and pray. Maybe I suggested it. I think it was Chris. I can't trust the memory of my double-booked mind. He had stronger faith and a deeper trust in the process, so I borrowed his confidence and decided to walk things out as they unfolded.

Chris talked about his oldest daughter, Anna, who just graduated high school and was heading off to *Link,* a Christian gap-year program in Missouri. We talked about his upcoming summer schedule: two youth camps followed by leading a mission trip to Southeast Asia. Chris used to travel as a missionary prior to his pastorate at CrossBridge. He's been to over 50 countries and preached in countless cities.

We talked about the "creature comforts" of America. Chris remembered when Anna was a baby and Ann Marie picked him up from his ministry/mission work in the Congo. On the ride home from the airport, she stopped at a large retailer store in San Antonio to run in for some items. Chris waited in their car since Anna had fallen asleep. His body was on a different time clock. His mind was on overload. Everything about his current situation was virtually science-fiction to the folks in the Congo. Air conditioning? They don't have it. Huge retail stores loaded with all the goods you could ever imagine? They wouldn't believe it. A climate-controlled car with a baby in a specialized, manufacturer's guaranteed, safety-tested car seat? They would be astonished.

Chris reminisced to me about how he sat in the parking lot and watched people go by. Americans: clean, well-fed, well-washed, perfumed and primped, parking expensive cars on freshly paved parking lots, rushing in for basketfuls of items they would buy with plastic credit cards to take back home to their brick homes in gated communities. Those items would be placed on polished granite countertops and then arranged neatly in their paneled cupboards or large pantries. There was so much food. Chris remembers his head spinning at the disparity. I forgot to ask him what he ate in the Congo. I forgot to ask him a lot of questions about the Congo.

I learned so much from my deployment to Afghanistan. I was glad I went. It made me feel like a real soldier. I never felt more like a soldier than when I was hungry, tired, dirty, and weapon-clad. Just then I'd remembered something I'd heard. I told it to Chris as a quote, but fumbled it. It was something about how the Holy Spirit comforts us, but not to *make* us comfortable.

I wondered if Chris felt more like a Christian when he was preaching in the Congo than when he was preaching to the middle and upper-class folks in San Antonio. I asked him that. He said it can be hard for pastors and missionaries to come home from overseas because of the strangeness of the contrast: almost a let-down to return to the land of plenty. The gap between need and plenty is too much to process. I mentioned that it's that way for military members coming home from deployment, too.

I wanted to tell Chris of the shopping trip to the North-Star mall that Barry and the boys and I took just three days after my return from Afghanistan. We were buying clothes for our niece's upcoming wedding in Pennsylvania. The big day was just two weeks away, and we would see all of our extended family members. Barry bought me a new dress. I felt uncomfortable. I acted grateful.

Leaving the mall, on the way to our van, Barry kicked a small manhole cover that was ajar. It shifted into place making a loud metallic sound. I ducked, throwing my hands over my head, and hit the deck. Josh and William laughed nervously. Barry stared, shocked. I recovered to a stand feeling embarrassed. We rode home with the radio off for many miles. I forgot to tell Chris that. Coming home can be hard. Trying to describe it can be even harder.

Reflections & A Tune
Not that I speak in regard to need, for I have learned in whatever state I am, to be content: I know how to be abased, and I know how to abound. Everywhere and in all things I have learned both to be full and to be hungry, both to abound and to suffer need. (Philippians 4:11-12)
And whatever you do, do it heartily, as to the Lord and not to men, knowing that from the Lord you will receive the reward of the inheritance; for you serve the Lord Christ. (Colossians 3:23-24)
You therefore must endure hardship as a good soldier of Jesus Christ. No one engaged in warfare entangles himself with the affairs of this life, that he may please him who enlisted him as a soldier. (2 Timothy 3-4)
Song Recommendation: "Speak Life" by Toby Mac

Conversation Starters

- How does "having too many minds" affect you?

- Have you ever worked on a large project with someone and had to collaborate and communicate your way through the maze of project development? Share your experience.

- What is the farthest distance you've traveled from home? What was your return like?

- Do you know a Christian missionary or a military veteran? Share about a conversation you've had with him or her.

8 - Number Our Days

> "Isn't it funny how day by day nothing changes,
> but when you look back, everything is different…"
>
> C.S. Lewis

2018 was an "everything-is-different" year for me. In May, June, and July of 2017, my oldest son turned 18, graduated from high school, and left home for military service, respectively. A milestone every month. Two months after Josh left, I retired from the Army. I was a little clingy to 2017, as I sorted out how to be a stay-at-home mom in a house filled with that someone-is-missing quietness. Things were as lopsided as a three-legged, square table. So, it was no surprise that I was still writing 2017 when the calendar said 2018. Thankfully, the third weekend in February lifted my emotional fog and shifted me in a forward-looking direction.

The annual "Winter Retreat" for the Ablaze Ministry was February 16-18, at Highland Lakes, in Spicewood, Texas. The theme of the weekend was *Stranger Things* (based on the television show set in the 1980s). Nostalgia for days gone by extended decades prior to 2017, as I searched the local thrift stores for a vintage outfit for the 1980s dance party scheduled for Saturday night. I planned to show my tenth-grade life group girls just how big Miss Katie's hair could get. Thank you, pink foam rollers and Rave® Hairspray!

The Friday night message was on Psalm 90, the only psalm of Moses. The entire thing is packed with power. As the Holy Spirit moved during Chris' teaching, I loosened my grip on 2017 and on all my past days. Chris exposed multiple truths from the 17-line psalm. He drew our attention to verse 12:

"So teach us to number our days,
That we may gain a heart of wisdom".

True to form, Chris had visual aids. He started with a video from twelve years prior of him and his two adorable toddler-aged girls; his little munchkins as he called them. They were so young and cute on the video. Since his girls were now teenagers and in attendance at the

Winter Retreat, his point was well taken: Time Flies. (I choked back tears.)

In Psalm 90, Moses looked back to the *beginning* of time, and *before* time, to speak of God's eternal existence, outside of time. God's eternal existence contrasts with our limited existence. Our Creator has no beginning and no end. We have both a beginning *and* an end. Chris had us turn to the person next to us and say, "Hey! You were made from dust!" This was instantly humbling and marvelous, and brought many nervous giggles from the teens. Chris moved us straight to Moses' prayer in verse 12: "teach us to number our days." Teach us! (We need to be taught!). LORD, teach us to number our days. Our future days. You have ordained each one.

Chris showed images on the overhead screen of grid-paper boxes and X's in the boxes, each X representing a single day. He showed slides depicting how many days were left until certain major life events. He went through how many days were left until the students graduated from high school. I locked onto the number of days left for my youngest son, William: 837 days. A lump formed in my throat. A message formed in my brain: *Katie! Wake up! Stop looking back to 2017. Make the most of these days before BOTH your boys are out of the house!* Chris went through several life milestones: average days until the student graduates from college, gets married, and becomes a parent. Mercy! I was getting his message loud and clear. It was as if the very act of numbering these days was doing exactly what Moses' prayer requested: "that we may gain a heart of wisdom." I felt wisdom blow through my spirit like an industrial fan blowing out the melancholy dust I had collected by staring backward rather than forward in time.

Chris returned to the beginning of Psalm 90 to reiterate God's existence outside of time. Moses poetically expressed:

> Lord, You have been our dwelling place in all generations.
> Before the mountains were brought forth, Or ever
> You had formed the earth and the world,
> Even from everlasting to everlasting,
> You are God."

Those lines give us an expansive view of God. Chris said he dared not attempt to demonstrate the contrast between God's bigness and our smallness. There isn't a small enough object to mark our smallness nor a big enough object to mark God's juxtaposed bigness.

Instead, Chris told of when he was a skinny 13-year-old at the beginning of the summer between his 8th and 9th grade school years. Eager to play football in high school, he was ready to actively build muscle bulk. His dad bought him a bench and weights for lifting. One day, shortly after having the workout equipment, Chris's dad came into the garage where he was working out and asked, "How many pounds do you think I can bench press?" Given that challenging question, Chris admitted to seeing his dad as old and weak. Chris's dad, wiser than Chris imagined, and stronger than he ever let on, instructed Chris to put ALL the plates on the bar and to move over so he could have a go. Chris was astonished by his dad's strength, and even more astonished at his endurance when he continued, rep after rep, without fatigue! Chris was amazed at his father's ability and quickly saw how wrongly he had pegged his dad as old and weak. Simultaneously, Chris realized how much work he had left to do in the weight training department to catch up to "old Pops." Chris's story captured the all-too-common, similar error we make with our Heavenly Father. We wrongly perceive that we are *more* capable, *more* relevant, *more* skilled than God. It is noteworthy (and shameful) how easily we drift into this double-sided error. Side one: God is not as big as He truly is. Side two: I am bigger than I really am.

There are two, often repeated themes to Chris's teaching. Theme number one is that God is much bigger than we can fathom. Theme number two is, and I will directly quote Chris here, "It's not about you." How refreshing for a youth pastor to give students the truth, despite it being an unpopular message. When Chris said, "What I am *desperate* for you to understand is that we have an incredible capacity to make ourselves the center of everything that happens on earth," my own heart swelled with the same sentiment. The reason he is desperate for the students to understand this (and me too) is that making ourselves the center of our existence comes with an unexpected and incredibly heavy burden, one we don't have to bear.

Tears for Fears had a chart-topping song in the Eighties called "Everybody Wants to Rule the World," exposing man's desire to be sovereign over himself. Does the popularity of the song reflect the unpopularity of the truth of God's established authority? Look closely. Our culture sells the same, antiquated lie Satan told Eve. That lie says, "Follow and fulfill your own desire, and you can be *like* God." Many take that bait and are ensnared in the "me-centered" (humanistic) worldview that tempts us to be *like* God: masters of our universe.

The corrupt belief that grows from the lie that we can be *like* God is that life *IS* all about us. Look at the social media platforms with the "selfie" photographs, status and profile updates, and blogging (and now vlogging) our day-to-day mundane experiences. See how disoriented we have become. At their best, social media creates a fantasy that life IS all about me! At their worst, they create a counterfeit version of "being known." Call it notoriety, popularity, validation, or harmless recognition, but when sought from our fellow man, they fall flat, empty, and ironically kick the door wide open for spiritual trouble to enter. Whitney Houston's successful song of 1985 was wrong! Learning to love myself is *not* the greatest love of all. Moses had it right in his only song (psalm): it is God who has been our dwelling place for all generations. *God's* love is the greatest love of all.

When we don't know and believe that God is our dwelling place and rest contentedly and joyfully with Him, we mistakenly place ourselves in the center of our existence and lash about wildly dissatisfied. We work ourselves into a stress ball state of worldly wealth and accumulations only to end up physically exhausted, miserable in relationships, emotionally empty, and spiritually desperate. No social popularity can fulfill us, for we were made for communion with our Creator, God. Psalm 90, verse 14 speaks of the value of coming to know God while we are young: "Oh, satisfy us early with Your mercy, That we may rejoice and be glad all our days!" Christ's followers gain a heart of wisdom by numbering our days and seeking God early in our lives so we can be satisfied *daily* by His mercies.

The message on numbering our days was a reality check that automatically ushered in wisdom. The "number our days" prayer generated a rich life group that evening as the sophomore high school girls and I gathered for discussion. We talked about the benefit of developing the perspective of God as bigger than us. One girl, Hannah, talked about wanting to know that she doesn't have to be her own mini-god; she shared how impossible is has been to keep control over the things in her life. She heard freedom in the message of being made of dust by a God who was never made by anyone. Interestingly, we subconsciously hyper-idealize one another and erect impossible standards of perfection for ourselves. To hear that we are each made of, and will one day return to, the ground substance of dust is liberating! Run to your Bible and read Psalm 103. See the spectacular lines of verses 14-16: "For He (God) knows our frame; He remembers that we are dust. As for man, his days are like grass; As a flower of the field, so he flourishes. For the wind passes over it, and it is gone, And its place remembers it no more." I love it! God remembers that we are dust. At Winter Retreat, Chris reminded us that God remembers. When we know who God is and we know who we are (in Him), we get our feet on solid, spiritual ground. Simply put: He is the creator; we are the created.

Chris offered a spiritual health assessment. Ask yourselves, "Do you fear God? Do you stand amazed at His greatness?" Do you stand in reverence of God in His rightful place as your Creator and Sustainer? The second self-inventory strategy is to gauge our relationship with sin. "Do you hate sin? Do you turn from the presence of sin?"

Another girl in life group, Lauren (shy and contemplative) contributed the thought she had during the message, which was that being reconciled to God through Jesus Christ is a sacred gift bought at the highest price, which makes her reverent and thankful to be under God's ownership and management. She talked of freedom in Christ. I looked at the bright, young girls with gratitude. They were hearing transforming truth from God's word. I remembered reading something on a greeting card that said, "At this moment, you are both as old as you've ever *been* and as young as you'll ever *be*!" I was thankful, that at age fifteen, they knew the Lord. They were here at Winter Retreat investing time in growing in the grace and knowledge of Jesus Christ.

I asked the girls, "What does it really mean to have a heart of wisdom?" They surprised me with their deep answers. A wise heart doesn't waste time. A wise heart thinks about the outcome of his or her actions prior to acting. A wise heart considers the cost of an investment (of time or money). A wise heart is reliant upon God and crying out for the King of Kings to *"Teach us to number our days."* A wise heart is hungry for God's truth. A wise heart is a prayerful heart.

Numbering days requires reflection. Generally, I reflect at the end of December when I think ahead to upcoming year. I used to think a year was so long, but 365 days is actually not that many days. It has been over a year since the 2018 Winter Retreat, and I regularly think of Friday night's "*Number our Days*" message.

A fresh reminder came last week. I traveled to Pennsylvania for my Uncle Bill's funeral. I read chapter 15 of 1 Corinthians on the airplane there. This section of Scripture contains our gospel (v. 1-4), and tells what happens to our earthly bodies after death:

"It is sown a natural body, it is raised a spiritual body. There is a natural body, and there is a spiritual body. And so it is written, 'The first man Adam became a living being.' The last Adam became a life-giving spirit. However, the spiritual is not first, but the natural, and afterward the spiritual. The first man was of the earth, made of dust; the second Man is the Lord from heaven. As was the man of dust, so also are those who are made of dust; and as is the heavenly Man, so also are those who are heavenly. And as we have born the image of the man of dust, we shall also bear the image of the heavenly Man" (v.44-49).

Sitting in the church during the funeral, staring at the urn containing Uncle Bill's body, now in dust form after 62 years on earth, I prayed for fresh wisdom, "God, teach me to number *my* days." Maybe it was because I was back in my home state of Pennsylvania that I called to mind the prayer of the (deceased) Puritan preacher, Jonathan Edwards, who prayed, "Lord God, stamp eternity on my eyeballs." Edwards maintained a three-fold perspective: (a) life is short, (b) death is certain, and (c) eternity is forever.

Tonight, back home in San Antonio, I remember the life-giving power of last year's Winter Retreat. A photograph of me and William rocking our Eighties outfits hangs on the fridge. The life group girls were quite impressed by my "Big '80s Hair."

I am sitting here at my kitchen counter. William and his two teenage friends are raiding my pantry. They're bragging about their limitless appetites as they pile snack upon snack on a tray to take upstairs to hang out in what once was the boys' toy room. Oh, the numbering-days wisdom that keeps teaching me.

Tonight, I am blessed by a generous, expanding spirit and overwhelming joy for the presence of these three growing young men pouring Dr. Pepper into Texas-sized mugs. They are celebrating the last day of their eleventh-grade school year, which means they've got 366 days until high school graduation. Make 'em count, Boys! Make 'em count!

Reflections & A Tune
But we have this treasure in earthen vessels, that the excellence of the power may be of God and not of us. (2 Corinthians 4:7)
See then that you walk circumspectly, not as fools but as wise, redeeming the time, because the days are evil. (Ephesians 5:15-16)
But the LORD is in His holy temple. Let all the earth keep silence before him. (Habakkuk 2:20)
LORD, make me to know my end, And what is the measure of my days, That I may know how frail I am. Indeed, You have made my days as handbreadths, And my age is nothing before You; Certainly every man at his best state is but vapor. (Psalm 39:4-5)
Song Recommendation: "Almost Home" by Mercy Me

Conversation Starters

- How have you erred on either side of (a) God is not as big as He truly is or (b) I am bigger than I really am?

- How does contemplating your relatively short life affect you spiritually?

- What is one thing you will do as a result of soaking in the wisdom of Psalm 90?

- Tell about a memorable funeral service you've attended. What made it memorable?

9 -Sloppy Can of Worms

No Book Meeting. June 18

> "Good decisions come from experience.
> Experience comes from making bad decisions."
>
> Mark Twain

Chris and I didn't meet last week. He was at Passion Camp with a busload of teens. We couldn't meet this week either; he is in Dallas for another meeting. Speaking of meetings, I had a business meeting last Friday. It went sideways pretty fast when new facts emerged. Shocking facts, actually. So now my husband and I will not be buying a franchise. I should have known something was fishy with the current franchise owner. Friday's meeting revealed things clearly. I should have seen it coming, except that I totally missed it. I do that. I miss things. I see what I want to see. A therapist friend of mine calls it "malignant optimism." My husband just calls me *gullible*. I don't like the word *gullible*. My sister, Kristen, got tricked into looking up *gullible* in the Dictionary because someone told her it wasn't in there. Boy, was Krissy gullible!

Yesterday I had a lawyer meeting. I got the lawyer two weeks ago because I started to sense something was wrong with the franchise deal. I like the lawyer. The meetings with her are nice. She is smart and very funny with lots of clever sayings. Her office is gorgeous with a city view. She told me today that the franchise deal was a sloppy can of worms. I laughed and wrote *sloppy can of worms* in my notebook. I asked her about it. She said she got the phrase from her dad's mom who was her favorite grandma. She called it a colloquialism. I wrote that down too because I had forgotten all about the word "*colloquialism.*" She grew up in Georgia, outside of Atlanta. The grandma, not my lawyer. The lawyer was an Army Brat. She moved a lot as a kid. I wondered if my own boys are mad that they moved a lot. I asked her if her grandma was still alive. She said she was not and neither was her dad who retired from the Army and is buried in the Fort Sam Houston cemetery. She visits him. She doesn't have to visit her grandma because she keeps her grandma's ashes in a vase in her living room. Her grandma, when she was alive, told her about Jesus and how He was the light of the world who came to save us. I wanted to tell her about Chris and Psalm 90 and Ablaze and Winter Retreat, but I just sat there.

I listened as she unpacked the sloppy can of worms and pointed out the writing on the wall that the business deal was as dead as a door-knob. I am writing in colloquialisms to honor the lawyer's grandma from Georgia. I never asked what her name was. When I got home from the fancy lawyer's office, I emailed the franchise owner to tell her that the deal was off and that I wished her all the best. I started to cry. I guess I *am* gullible. I wanted it to work out for me and my husband to have a business to run together. Disappointment tears came fast and hot like a flood on my face. No one else was home so the timing was perfect for the flood. I was starting to feel angry inside, especially because the franchise owner wrote back to my email. She was dumbstruck that I was canceling the deal. I was dumbstruck that *she* was dumbstruck. She *knew* what she *knew* all along and didn't tell *me* until last Friday.

I paced from my back door to my front door, wringing my hands, astonished in my mind as the storm inside me raged and the flood on my face continued. My eleven-year old Labrador retriever knew something was wrong. He senses things. He paced with me. Back door. Front door. He would rally his energy if I needed to walk things off. I do that. Walk things off. It works. I bet the lawyer's grandma used to tell her dad to walk things off. Moms usually tell their sons to walk things off. My mind was unsteady, like a twisted, matted ball of knitting yarn — the harder I tried to straighten it out, the tighter the knots. I momentarily stopped crying. I emailed Chris and Ann Marie. I didn't want to tell Barry about the email reply from Mrs. Dumbstruck, yet. He was in Pennsylvania tending to his Pops who was quickly declining in health. I feared the word gullible might come up.

Chris and Ann Marie knew about the business deal. I reached out for prayer and wisdom and guidance. I was a cast-down sheep in need of my shepherding pastor. In the email I asked Chris if it was OK to pray a fiery Psalm toward a specific person. I was thinking of Psalm 35, which I have previously prayed in a desperate, loud voice while *specifically* thinking of a *specific* person. *Specifically*, that the angel of the LORD would chase and pursue.

A cast sheep is one who wanders off from the flock, finds a soft divot to lie down in, and accidentally flips upside down, unable to recover to a standing position without help. David, the shepherd king, knew about sheep being cast — that's why he wrote in the Psalms about his soul being cast down within him. That's what happened to me after the lawyer meeting and the email reply. My soul got cast down. I was upside down, bleating, flailing, feeling far from the flock and seeking a shepherd's rescue. Ann Marie texted me straight away, with emojis. (There is *something* about her loving emojis.) She told me Chris was away but he would reach out. She said to call her anytime. She asked if I wanted to talk. I texted that I couldn't because I was too tearful. Tears are as uncomfortable to me as fitted dresses. She understood. She said that I was loved. I knew she was right. I knew it in my head, but my heart felt like a gullible matted ball of yarn sunk inside a sloppy can of worms holding a dead doorknob.

I power walked my dog, tears streaming. I kept my earbuds in to send the message to my neighbors that I couldn't visit. Normally, I visit. Not tonight. I learned this "ignore me please" earbud sign from observing teenagers. They know about the volcanic underpinnings of emotions. They're experts. I suddenly felt the urge to pray for my Ablaze life group girls. They're fourteen and fifteen and have lots of feelings. I prayed Psalm 35 against all the darkness that threatens the teens. I asked God to plead their cause and strive with those who strive with them and to release them from destructions and lion-like enemy attacks. Praying for them pulled me out of the quick sand of self-pity.

The next morning, I went to the post office to mail Mrs. Dumbstruck back her franchise materials. It was the lawyer's idea to send it through certified mail. It seemed a sophisticated strategy, outside of my nature, but I was paying her to make clear-minded decisions on my behalf, so there I was in the post-office. My heart pounded and my hands shook as I tried to work the monstrous sized, complex tape dispenser the postmaster handed me to tape up the box.

In God's perfect timing, my cell phone chimed. I welcomed the distraction, dug through my purse, and looked at my phone. It was a text from Chris. He said he was in Dallas but would make himself free to talk, and he was so sorry for the franchise deal going sour. He said he was praying. This, I just knew, was true. Knowing Chris was praying galvanized me to finish taping the box. I walked to the counter as Patty, the clerk, called me forward. Her suspiciousness emerged, "You're only mailing this *across town*? You need them to *sign* for it?"

I felt the squishiness of sloppy worms. I nodded, agitated at her implied judgment. "That's correct. Across town. Certified." As I inhaled and tried to focus, I glanced around, and about one foot to my left stood an older gentleman I recognized from church. Barry and I stand behind him each week. I immediately pictured his worship hands raised high in praise. He smiled a calm, supportive smile as if to say, "walk it off." Two days ago, this man had won the Father's Day gift at church for having been a father the longest. His son was forty-nine. When he went forward to receive the gift card, Pastor Brian mentioned that he is a dedicated prayer warrior. That day in the post office, we met formally. He shook my hand so kindly. I knew those hands were praying hands.

I also knew that Chris's text message from moments ago and this saintly, prayerful, father-man were God's signs that His ministering angels were ushering reinforcement to the spiritual battleground in my heart. My tangled heart was fighting as I stood inside the post office, searching for truth and peace and wisdom and strength to move on.

Patty was waiting for my credit card. Mr. Prayer Warrior made quick work of telling her about our church. He invited her. He pointed to us to point out that she already knew two people who went there. Patty smiled generously. As I walked out of the post office, clutching the receipt to save for my tax records, I felt the flood waters of my grief subside. I felt a rainbow spreading over my soul. Suddenly, it dawned on me that Jesus is never dumbstruck. He knows exactly what He's doing. I recommitted to trust things to Jesus. I made a fresh surrender, a fresh start.

Reflections & A Tune

Do not remember the former things,
Nor consider the things of old.
Behold, I will do a new thing,
Now it shall spring forth;
Shall you not know it?
I will even make a road in the wilderness
And rivers in the desert. (Isaiah 43:18-19)

Plead my cause, O LORD, with those who strive with me;
Fight against those who fight against me.
Take hold of shield and buckler,
And stand up for my help.
Also draw out the spear,
And stop those who pursue me.
Say to my soul, "I am your salvation." (Psalm 35:1-2)

Show me Your ways, O LORD;
Teach me Your paths.
Lead me in Your truth and teach me,
For you are the God of my salvation;
On You I wait all the day. (Psalm 25:4-5)

Depart from evil and do good;
Seek peace and pursue it.
The eyes of the LORD are on the righteous,
And His ears are open to their cry. (Psalm 34:14-15)

Song Recommendation: "Known" by Tauren Wells

Conversation Starters

- When have you faced an unexpected disappointment (loss of a dream)?

- How do you feel after a long walk and a good cry? Do you have a dog? What does he/she do when you are visibly upset?

- Have you experienced a wink from God by a person texting you or showing up in a location just when you needed someone?

- Are you familiar with the imprecatory Psalms? Have you prayed them in any situation?

10 - It's Just Pickles

"In the last analysis, a pickle is a cucumber with experience."
Irena Chalmers

Chris doesn't like pickles. If he suspects that those thin, tangy, former-cucumber slices have touched the buttery bun of his Chick-fil-A sandwich, he stands in line to request a new sandwich. Chris was meeting a friend for lunch at Chick-fil-A. He ordered his standard meal: chicken sandwich, hold the pickles, waffle fries, and a Dr. Pepper. He got to his seat, unfolded the foil-lined wrapper to stage his meal. Just to be sure, he opened his sandwich and saw two green pickles. No problem. This happens (that's why he checks). He packed the sandwich back into the foil wrapper and walked to the counter. He kindly told the young server about the sandwich error and handed over the pickled one. He returned to his seat. The server brought him a new sandwich. Great! The fries were still hot. Chris opened the sandwich to realize that all the server did was remove the pickles. Chris could see the faint, slightly green imprint from where the pickles had been. Now, with less patience, Chris emphatically wrapped up the sandwich and hustled back to the counter. As he stood there in hunger-fueled frustration, his ears tuned into the deep voice of the person ahead of him in line. That deep voice aggressively berated the young man behind the counter for a similar food-order error. Chris felt the Holy Spirit's recognizable influence on his own spirit in a gentle correction with, *Sit back down, Chris. It's just pickles.* Obediently, Chris returned to his seat.

At Ablaze on Wednesday, Chris told of his Holy Spirit "it's just pickles" experience. He was teaching chapter 14 of Romans which instructs, "As for the one who is weak in faith, welcome him, but not to quarrel over opinions. One person believes he may eat anything, while the weak person eats only vegetables. Let not the one who eats despise the one who abstains, and let not the one who abstains pass judgment on the one who eats, for God has welcomed him. Who are you to pass judgment on the servant of another? It is before his own master that he stands or falls. And he will be upheld, for the Lord is able to make him stand."

Before that night, I'd never thought about Romans 14. *And*, I never realized that the chapter is *entirely* about the Christians in Rome who were quarreling about rules, mostly rules about whether it is acceptable to eat meat. There *is* a short segment about the Sabbath: Romans 14:5-6a, but mostly it's a chapter about eating.

Chris explained the historical background of why Paul was writing to the Romans about eating. It turns out that people were selling choice meat that had been sacrificed to idols and there was a debate about whether it was lawful to buy and eat that meat. Romans 14 was starting to make sense, and I could appreciate the eat-versus-abstain issue. I had a momentary image of me back in the first century. Would I have been a carefree meat eater or a *where-it-came-from matters* abstainer? Perhaps, the better question, and the question Chris was alluding to, is would I have quarreled with those who held the opposing view?

In Chris's Chic-Fil-A story, pickles represent personal preference. The Holy Spirit that whispered a gentle correction to Chris telling him to sit down and not be argumentative about pickles (or leftover pickle juice on a bun) was the *same* Holy Spirit Who had guided Paul to write this message in Romans 14. And notice that the message was the same: do not be side-tracked by irrelevant issues.

No one wins. Chris went on to share about a time in college when he'd traveled some distance on a bus to a church event. He and his buddies spent a night at someone's uncle's house, and they decided to pool their money and order pizza. What should have been an easy task of figuring out how many to get and what toppings to add turned into an ordeal and escalated into a stalemate. Someone wanted pineapple on the pizza, and no one else did. The fight escalated into a power struggle fueled by the one who had more money to demand his preferences be honored above the others. Chris expressed the confusion about how quickly the former unity of their brotherhood unraveled. He explained that their love for one another, peace in their interactions, and generosity of spirit declined. The cloud of annoyance hung heavy the morning after the pizza battle which darkly shadowed the trip. It wasn't until late afternoon the next day of the trip that the young men talked it out and reconciled. This disunity of a single evening of a long-ago trip grieved Chris's memory which holds a lesson for him (and every one of us at Ablaze). Pickles and pineapples were making Romans 14 come to life.

Paul's corrective message continues:

> But why do you judge your brother? Or why do you show contempt for your brother? For we shall all stand before the judgment seat of Christ.
> For it is written:
> 'As I live, says the LORD,
> Every knee shall bow to Me,
> And every tongue shall confess to God.'

So then each of us shall give account of himself to God. Therefore let us not judge one another anymore, but rather resolve this, not to put a stumbling block or a cause to fall in our brother's way." (Romans 14:10:13)

In matters of truth we must stand resolute, but in matters of preference, we sit in peace and allow personal choice. This is not to be mistaken for a soft-serve Christianity, or what some experts have termed "The Customized Christ" movement. For we know that God doesn't change His mind, and that He is the same yesterday, today, and tomorrow. He shows no partiality and will judge perfectly.

Romans 14 is a warning against the all-too-common tendency to turn the pursuit *of* truth, and journey *in* truth, into a list of do's and don'ts. Flattening Christianity out like this automatically creates the categorizing of "those-who-do" and "those-who-don't" and that always leads to man judging man. We are so prone to look on, observe, and judge one another's behaviors, all the while knowing in our deepest selves that we are far from perfect. Doing this is the birthing ground of religion and it is a sure-fire way to destroy true spirituality, more specifically, a life devoted to God through His Son Jesus Christ.

Chris's sermon on Romans 14 is a collector's seashell for me because through this teaching, the Holy Spirit enlightened my understanding of a snare that is organic to humanness. That is the snare of judgment. Oh, it can be harmless enough. I have my viewpoint, my opinion, my beliefs, my preferences. You have yours. We both think we are right. Pickles on sandwiches. Pineapples on pizza.

As a child I used to watch a television show called *The People's Court*. As Chris unpacked Romans 14, I daydreamed a scene from that old courtroom where those in favor of eating the meat sacrificed to idols opposed those who took issue with their lackadaisical meat buying.

My mind created this scene:

First, the prosecution. "Your careless actions are despicable. Do you know what it means to buy and eat the meat that was sacrificed to idols? How dare you disrespect the one true God by waving your disloyalty around like a freedom banner to sin? We wouldn't dare act in a way that might be disloyal to God."

Meanwhile the defendants, shaking their heads... aghast... not listening to the concerns of the prosecution but chomping at the bit to get up and explain away their meat buying.

When they get their chance to talk, they say, "We know this meat was sacrificed to idols. Who cares? Idols have no power over us. We need to eat. We are hungry. We believe in the one true God who gives us every morsel of every bite we take of sacrificed and unsacrificed foods. We have faith in God to know that he will bless us and nourish us through this meat, regardless of what the pagans believe. It's just food. God dropped manna from the sky for 40 years, so He obviously knows we need to eat. Why should we not eat this choice meat?"

You see, both sides claim to have God's support for their position.

As Chris closed his message, I picture the judge in my make-believe courtroom case declaring to both parties, "It's just pickles. It's just pineapple. Why are you all quarreling against one another so ferociously?"

Thursday, the day after Ablaze, William and I read Paul's letter to the Colossians. There is a nice buildup as Paul tells the church members at Colossi that they were alive with Christ, forgiven of all their trespasses, and that their record of debt with its legal demands had been canceled by Jesus. Paul goes on to tell how Jesus disarmed the rulers and authorities and put them to open shame by triumphing over them. And then, there is this awkward transition to Paul warning them to not judge one another. Well, I always thought it was awkward until that night at Ablaze. Here is what Paul tells them, "Therefore let no one pass judgment on you in question of food and drink, or with regard to a festival or a new moon or a Sabbath. These are a shadow of the things to come, but the substance belongs to Christ" (Colossians 2:16-17).

So, I now understood the link of being forgiven followed by the very logical and necessary warning to avoid passing judgment on a brother or sister in Christ. There was almost an echo in my heart that reverberated the words of truth, *"the substance belongs to Christ."*

There is a rise of divisiveness over cultural issues, and I must be so careful not to cling to either side of an argument. I pictured people arguing about a political issue and imagined the spiritual forces behind them in a taunting fashion, egging on the quarrels and debates, not specifically caring about which side was right, or where the truth actually was, but rather just demonic cheerleading over the fighting and frustration of one side against the other. Our adversary, who crawls around like a lion, wants to keep us focused on rules rather than relationships. That swift flash of spiritual understanding quickened my spirit to regroup under the banner of God's love.

Chris closed his sermon that night with the thesis of the Romans 14 (v.16-18), "Therefore do not let your good be spoken of as evil; for the kingdom of God is not eating and drinking, but righteousness and peace and joy in the Holy Spirit. For he who serves Christ in these things is acceptable to God and approved by men."

I wrote down the words Righteousness, Peace, and Joy. My doodling pen kept outlining the R, the P, and the J. I started thinking of a rocket propelled grenade: RPG. In my military career as a therapist, who specialized in traumatic limb amputations, I witnessed (and treated) horrific destruction caused by RPGs. I thought of the spiritual RPGs that Romans 14 warned against. Without knowing it, Chris uncovered the bomb diffuser hidden in Romans: it has been there all along: RPJ: Righteousness, Peace, and Joy. Right now, as I type this, I am thinking about the powerful, healing trifecta of the RPJ and praying a blessing over all my former patients who lost limbs to RPGs. Every time I put a pickle on a chicken sandwich or a pineapple on a pizza, I plan to remember Romans 14 and recommit to only throwing RPJs. In case you wondered, I am pro-pickle and pro-pineapple.

Reflections & A Tune

All things are lawful for me, but all things are not helpful. All things are lawful for me, but I will not be brought under the power of any. Foods for the stomach and the stomach for foods, but God will destroy both it and them. (1 Corinthians 6:12-13)

Therefore, if food makes my brother stumble, I will never again eat meat, lest I make my brother stumble. (1 Corinthians 8:13)

Therefore, whether you eat or drink, or whatever you do, do all to the glory of God. (1 Corinthians 10:31)

But He answered and said, "It is written, 'Man shall not live by bread alone, but by every word that proceeds from the mouth of God.' (Matthew 4:4)

Song Recommendation: "Come As You Are" by Crowder

Conversation Starters

- When is a time that you recently struggled with judging someone for his/her decisions? How did you process it? Were you able to let it go?

- Why do you suppose we are so prone to judge one another in small and large things in this life?

- What is one way you can commit to infuse righteousness, peace, and joy into your relationships?

- Do you like pickles on your Chic Fil-A sandwich? What about pineapple on your pizza?

11 - Calipari

> "I kept always two books in my pocket,
> one to read, one to write in."
>
> Robert Louis Stevenson

Chris and I met today. He leaves in a few days for Southeast Asia. He is the leader of a group of missionaries from CrossBridge. Ann Marie and their girls are going too. They'll be gone for a few weeks. I could feel his energy and momentum for the journey. He must have had a sizeable, pre-trip to-do list, but thankfully our book meeting was still a "go." Eager for feedback, I wanted his outlook on the draft I had emailed him last week.

Chris had read what I wrote so far. Now he knows about the seashells. He said he was humbled and in awe of the work the Holy Spirit does *with* and *through* his life's work at Ablaze. He was also humbled by how I had been impacted by his ministry. We talked about the mysterious, purifying power of the Holy Spirit. I had not yet told Chris how much Ablaze had restored in my life. I may tell him later, if ever.

Over the years in ministry, Chris would occasionally pass out paper and pens for students, encouraging them to jot down their thoughts during his teaching. I've witnessed him use this strategy in Ablaze. Without fail, after the students leave for the evening, he finds a few left-behind papers. In search of a student's name, Chris looks and reads. He told me this today. I would do the same. More often than not, he said, there's no name, just the scribblings of sermon notes. Reading the students' reflections is a glimpse at the answer to every pastor's pondering of "Is what I *said* what they *heard*?" Preaching is not chemistry, so both sides of the equation don't balance.

Chris said reading what I wrote for our book was a version of him finding someone's sermon notes. Incidentally, he told me his Mom always took good sermon notes. I liked knowing that. One of my nicknames in the Army was "*Mama K*." I suppose taking thorough notes when the pastor is teaching *does* seem like a responsible mom thing to do.

An Army chaplain once told me that Christians need strong backs, sharp minds, and soft hearts. Writing sermon notes keeps my mind sharp. The indwelling Holy Spirit softens my heart when the sword of the Spirit, which is the word of God, is heard, received, understood, and studied. Reviewing my sermon notes days later seems to strengthen my resolve to live out my destined purpose in God's kingdom.

Chris felt that our book was about discipleship: the process of following Jesus and walking with people going the same way. Jesus is *the Way*. Maturing in His word through listening and learning is part of walking in the Way. Eugene Peterson's book title fittingly describes discipleship as, "A long obedience in the same direction."

Discipleship. That word sunk deep in my mind. It resonated. I thought about how a *growing* faith *is* a *strengthening* faith. I pictured my potted tree in front of the window in my home office. It's medium sized. (The tree, not my office.) In 2015, my parents escaped the long, harsh Pennsylvania winter and spent several months with us in sunny San Antonio. The tree was a home décor spruce-up prior to their arrival. Because of the shiny blue planter pot, I named the tiny six-inch tree "Calipari "after John Calipari, the University of Kentucky men's basketball coach. Calipari is from Moon Township, a suburb of Pittsburgh. He graduated from Clarion University, as did Barry, both his sisters, and two of my three sisters. I had just read Coach Cal's book and was nostalgic for my graduate school days in Lexington. I used to paint my boys' faces blue and white and take them to games. So, I named the baby tree "Calipari" and watered and pruned it faithfully. That little tree has coached me right along.

Over the past few years I noticed that as Calipari grows in height, the branches get thicker and stronger, and there are many more leaves and sprouts. Interestingly, I have never actually witnessed Calipari grow, and yet somehow, it has. It's well over two feet tall now. Come to think of it, the same thing happened to Josh and William, growing tall and strong when I wasn't looking.

Discipleship is growing tall and strong in the Spirit. Chris's perspective made me excited that this book project might fulfill the vision God had given. Discipleship. Yes. Discipleship captures the singularity of devotion to Christ, attentiveness to the growing process, and the accelerating power of being a sheep willing to eat from green pastures planted with truth by faithful, shepherding teachers.

From a bird's view this book meeting was monumental. From a worm's view, this book meeting was helpful too because I asked Chris *specific* questions about the draft. Had I misinterpreted anything he said? Does he, in fact, order Dr. Pepper at Chick Fil A? And, will you please clarify what it means in the second chapter of Revelation when Jesus talks disapprovingly about the churches that ate things sacrificed to idols? I wondered about this last thing because I didn't want to mislead anyone when I wrote up the chapter from my sermon notes on Romans 14.

Chris clarified. To his knowledge, nothing had been misinterpreted in what I wrote so far. (Sigh of relief!). Yes, Dr. Pepper. (I thought so!). And then Chris gave me a helpful exposition on Revelation chapter 2: Jesus is talking about idolatry *of the heart,* not idolatry of the mouth. Jesus always goes right to the heart. He always has, and He always will.

In chapter 2 of Revelation, Jesus mentions the churches of Pergamos and Thyatira. He points out their idolatry and names names: Balaam, Balak, and Jezebel. Jesus knows our hearts and *to whom* we pledge allegiance. We are always acting in allegiance to someone *or* something. The phrase of "eating things sacrificed to idols," found in Revelation chapter 2, is emblematic of end-times idolatry. That idolatry was present in early times too.

Chris gave me a history lesson. Back in the day, Israel insisted (through Samuel) to have a king. They didn't need a king. They had the ultimate King, Yahweh, but they wanted to be like the other nations. It was idolatry, misguided loyalty that came out of self-guided hearts. We still do this today: ignore the most holy trinity of Father, Son, and Holy Ghost and worship the unholy trinity of me, myself, and I. Chris taught quickly and effortlessly, drawing on his love for and knowledge of the scriptures.

When I got home from today's book meeting I looked up the history lesson. I found it in 1 Samuel, chapter 8. The elders of Israel were displeased that Samuel was old and his two sons, Joel and Abijah, who were judges, were sell-outs. Joel and Abijah had turned aside for what the Bible calls, "*dishonest gain.*" They also "*took bribes and perverted justice*" (v.3b). The Israelites were nervous and uncertain about their future, so they made a demand to Samuel:

"Look, you are old, and your sons do not walk in your ways. Now make us a king to judge us like all the nations." (v.5).

Samuel was upset. He prayed to the LORD. What happened next is interesting.

> And the LORD said to Samuel, "Heed the voice of the people in all that they say to you; for they have not rejected you, but they have rejected Me, that I should not reign over them. According to all the works which they have done since the day that I brought them out of Egypt, even to this day, with which they have forsaken Me an served other gods, so they are doing to you also. (v.7-8)

All day I've been thinking about the penetrating words that described Israel's treatment of God. They rejected God. They did not want to be under His reign. They forgot what slavery He had freed them from. They had forsaken him. They served other gods. It was a grim picture. It was no trouble for me to know exactly how they acted because for many years in my life, I was up to the same rejecting and forsaking and forgetting nonsense. This is the nonsense of serving other gods.

I took a walk around my neighborhood. I called Kristi in Pennsylvania. Today is her birthday and she's pregnant and expecting her first baby! It's a miracle! She wasn't home so I left her a message. I walked along and thought more about Chris's history lesson. I marveled about God absorbing the disloyalty of His people, His willingness to give them the king they wanted (but didn't need), His long-suffering, and then His grace in sending Jesus as the Spotless Lamb to atone for the treacherous infidelity of *all* men who believe and receive. I am glad Chris told me what he did about the second chapter of Revelation. It *revealed* much. The Spirit of truth, spoken through Chris, helped me tamp down my understanding of what I had previously meditated upon, *"the substance belongs to Christ."*

So, here I am this evening, circling back to Colossians 2 (v. 13-15), where Paul sums it up nicely:

> And you, being dead in your trespasses and the uncircumcision of your flesh, He has made alive together with Him, having forgiven you all trespasses, having wiped out the handwriting of requirements that was against us, which was contrary to us. And He has taken it out of the way, having nailed it to the cross. Having disarmed principalities and powers, He made a public spectacle of them, triumphing over them in it.

Reflections & A Tune
Not what goes into the mouth defiles a man; but what comes out of the mouth, this defiles a man. (Matthew 15:11)
For forty years I was grieved with that generation, And said, "it is a people who go astray in their hearts, And they do not know My ways. (Psalm 95:10)
But the LORD said to Samuel, "Do not look at his appearance or at his physical stature, because I have refused him. For the LORD does not see as man sees; for man looks at the outward appearance, but the LORD looks at the heart. (1 Samuel 16:7)
For you were like sheep going astray, but have now returned to the Shepherd and Overseer of your souls. (1 Peter 2:25)
Song Recommendation: "The Way" by Pat Barrett

Conversation Starters

- Are you in a discipleship relationship with a Christian brother or sister? If so, describe your experience: how frequently you meet and how it works.

- How is nurturing a spiritual life like taking care of a plant?

- In what ways have you made your spiritual life about rules and regulations rather than an intimate relationship with Jesus?

- How have you experienced God's patience with your wanderings? Give an example.

12 - I Need a Bag

> "He who sings scares away his woes."
>
> Cervantes

There was a special event at CrossBridge tonight. It was Bryan McCleery's album release party. Bryan is our worship pastor. He invited everyone to a free event to share his new songs.

A few days ago, I got an email from my friend, Sara. She used to live in San Antonio but married an Army guy and now lives in Alaska. Just like that. I know. The Army did that to me and my family for 20 years. One day you live here, and the next day you live there. On the upside, it's fun to move! On the downside, it's hard to move!

Sara sent an email to ask if I would befriend her friend, Harry. Harry is a single soldier (a medical supply technician) who was stationed in Fairbanks with Sara's husband, and they met him through their church. Harry was getting out of the Army and moving to San Antonio to start a new job. Of course, I would gladly welcome an Army brother and a Christian brother to San Antonio with open arms, so I agreed to Sara's friend request.

Ideally, I would have invited Harry over for dinner, but since I am not that into cooking fancy meals, or any meal really, (Barry does our cooking), I decided to just invite Harry to meet me at Bryan's free album release party. Harry agreed. Church lobby. Seven o'clock. Send a text when you're there. Which is exactly how it happened, except it wasn't just *me* who was waiting to meet Harry. Earlier in the week I got a text invitation from Mandy to sit with her at the concert. Mandy leads worship in our small life group, which meets in people's homes on Sunday nights. Mandy is also a photographer and writer. She didn't yet know that there wouldn't be any chairs. It was a standing concert! And it was standing room only! Also, with me and Mandy in the lobby, waiting for Harry, was Audry.

Audry and I served in the Army together at Walter Reed Army Medical Center in Washington, D.C. We were in Afghanistan together too, but at different operating bases, and I only saw her once. She and I have several friends in common and live a few miles apart in San Antonio, but we rarely see one another because of schedules. The last time we saw each other, not counting tonight's concert, was at a retirement party for a mutual friend. That was in January in Washington, D.C. Ironic how sometimes you have to travel a thousand miles to visit a neighbor.

Audry texted me an hour before the concert and asked if I was going to church on Sunday. She had visited once, about a year ago, and wanted to join me again. I told her I would not be at church on Sunday. I was traveling to Pittsburgh on Saturday for Kristi's baby shower. Kristi and Audry were friends too. I texted Audry about Bryan's free concert. She accepted the invitation, so there we were – me, Mandy, and Audry – three gals standing in the lobby, pre-concert, waiting to meet a friend of a friend

Harry arrived. We introduced ourselves and then found a spot to stand near the stage, not too near, and off to the left a little. We could see Bryan. We could read the lyrics on the large overhead screens:

> "Halleluiah. Highest praise.
> Name above all other names.
> Through earth and heaven, let it resound: He bore a cross, now
> He wears a crown.
> Lifted to the highest place, name above all other names."

I was connecting with a new friend through an old friend, an Army friend, and a life group friend – sisters and a brother in Christ – belting out truth. We united our voices with the others standing there – rekindling our joy in the Lord. What a firm foundation!

Occasionally, I could hear Mandy. She has a pitch-perfect, angelic voice. I was very happy to connect Harry with some folks at CrossBridge. I know all too well the disorientation of being the new person to a large city. It feels like someone just crushed your ten-thousand-piece Lego set and you have to start building it all over again.

My son, Josh, had been listening to, and loving, Bryan's album via a pre-release on Spotify. Suddenly I was overcome with a miss-my-kid sadness. Someone told me once that there's no distance in the spiritual realm. So, I took a few short video clips of Bryan singing, and texted Josh. The physical distance between San Antonio and San Diego evaporated as we connected on a spiritual wavelength. That felt good!

That wavelength is always powerful! Let me do it again! So, I asked Mandy to take a photograph of me, Harry, and Audry. I texted Sara so she could see us worshipping together. I added a few heart-eyed Emojis to let her know we missed her. Sara and Audry are friends from our Walter Reed days where Sara worked as a government civilian (she's a therapist, too). Since Sara and her family had just bid Harry a Fairbanks farewell a few days ago, I knew the photo would be fun for them in a may-the-circle-be-unbroken kind of way.

After several more songs, Bryan announced a brief intermission and invited folks to check out the merch table in the lobby. Merch is now the word for merchandise. Has texting culture done this? Vacation is vaca. A Bible study devotion is a devo. Adorable is adorbs. Favorite is fave; although, I think we can thank the 1970s for giving us fab from fabulous! Last week, William ventured to the grocery store on his own and admittedly almost missed the deli because he didn't realize that the large *delicatessen* sign was for the deli. We have a legit word prob here! Next time I will add guac to his shopping list and see what happens. This made me wonder if William knows that mayo is short for mayonnaise? Mrs. Lewis, my high school English teacher, used to tell me to write and speak in complete sentences. Now I wonder if she tells students to write and speak in complete words.

Tonight was Harry's last day in the Army, so after Bryan's concert, we celebrated his four years of honorable service with late night shakes at Sonic. I should have invited Mandy, but I assumed she had to get home to her three little ones. We sat at a picnic table outside of Sonic in the humid San Antonio air.

Audry told us about her upcoming retirement from the Army. She may move to Florida to live near her mom, Claudette, who is gearing up to fight her second battle against breast cancer. We talked about Audry's dad too. He lives in California and had a stroke and also needs help. Audry's sister lives near him. There is a certain comradery among military folks because we are usually stationed far away from our parents and siblings. And with the Lego sets of our lives being rebuilt every two to three years, it's hard to get traction and easy to feel adrift. I told them about "Poppie Bob," my elderly father-in-law, who recently moved to San Antonio to live with us since he can no longer live independently in his home in Pennsylvania. We shared our hearts and our sorrows and concerns.

Here we were, a make-shift family at an impromptu milkshake picnic. Three military members at different career junctures, united in faith and friendship. Worshipping earlier at the concert was so good for us and now as we sat outside Sonic, bearing each other's burdens, fulfilling the law of Christ.

I pledged to pray for Claudette. I told Audry and Harry that God hears and answers our prayers. And prayer changes us along the way. I didn't tell them about my bulletin board, but maybe one day I will tell, or even *show*, them. I have a bulletin board in Barry's and my bedroom. I put prayer requests of all kinds on it. I started three years ago after I saw the idea on the Internet.

When I am ironing, which I do every day, I look at my prayer board and talk to Jesus. He already knows, but I tell Him everything. I press out the wrinkles in Barry's work shirts. I press out my spiritual wrinkles. I make my requests known. Shirts and souls have a way of getting wrinkled from the wearing. And if your prayer request is on my board, I ask God to unkink your kinks too!

As Bryan McCleery's song lyrics go,

> "I know you are coming
> Faithful like the dawn.
> 'Til the whole world knows your name, all creation will proclaim: Our Hope Eternal, the reason for our song,
> Enduring Promise, He will right the wrong. He is faithful like the dawn."

Here is one of my recurring thoughts during my daily ironing: in 2001, I changed my self-centered mind (repented) and accepted the free gift of salvation through the shed blood of Jesus Christ and put all my trust in His finished work, and my spirit was born again. My born-again spirit is forever safe. Yet, some days I forget about eternity. Some days I don't act with the joy that eternal security brings me. It seems as though my soul (my mind, will, and emotions) still crinkles and creases. So, I claim my salvation and reassure myself that I am saved by grace through faith, and my spirit is sealed until the day of redemption when Christ returns. I anchor my spirit in hope, and then I get busy ironing out my crumpled soul through prayer.

Paul's call to action in Romans 12:2 is fitting: "And do not be conformed to the patterns of this world, but be transformed by the renewing of your mind, that you may prove what is that good, and acceptable, and perfect will of God."

Praying is like ironing as the heat and pressure of God's word is pressed into me through the Holy Spirit's power and presence. Praying brings transformational change where transformational change is needed, mostly in my wrinkled mind. My wayward will and shifting emotions need to be pressed out to align with God's good, acceptable, and perfect will. I like perfect. That is one of the reasons I like to iron. I like to unwrinkle wrinkled things. Since perfection is not obtainable while I am still in this earth suit, which the Bible calls "the flesh," I press on to the high calling of Christ. Prayer is the portal through which I press on.

During intermission at the concert tonight, I bought some merch. I bought William a shirt. I bought him a sticker, too. I bought Poppie a hat. I bought myself a CD (yes, old school!). I walked away happy with much merch and was looking forward to getting home and saying, "much merch" to William. He was on a first date and had to miss the concert. I was anticipating his eye-rolling "Oh Mom!!" William is a word nerd, too, so even though he may roll his eyes and say "Oh Mom!" I knew he'd like the ring of "much merch."

I realized that I didn't have a bag for the merch and my purse was already stuffed-to-bursting. That made me grumble. I felt an emotional wrinkle forming in my soul. I didn't want to walk out to my van before the concert ended. I didn't know what to do with my new stuff. I thought, *I need a bag! Why don't they bag the merch?*

Within ten seconds of my inner grumbling, Pastor Chris walked up to me and handed me a bag. "Hey Katie. This is from Ann Marie from our mission trip."

The bag was a gift bag with two lovely gifts from Lombok! I introduced Chris to Harry and Audry and smiled, thinking and praying in my spirit, "Well, that was fast, Jesus. I didn't even pray. I grumbled. Forgive me. And yet, you sent Pastor Chris to me with a bag, meeting my very immediate need, and a minor need at that!"

I stuffed my merch into the bag, and thanked Jesus for Pastor Chris's perfect timing. The gifts from Ann Marie are precious: a handcrafted bowl that is adorbs, and a small purse that is my new fave. This *is* a night I'll remember with my faith fam.

Reflections & A Tune

Praise the LORD with the harp; Make melody to Him with an instrument of ten strings. Sing to Him a new song; Play skillfully with a shout of joy. (Psalm 33:3)

If a son asks for bread from any father among you, will he give him a stone? Or if he asks for a fish, will give him a serpent instead of a fish? Or if he asks for an egg, will he offer him a scorpion? If you then, being evil, know how to give good gifts to your children, how much more will your heavenly Father give the Holy Spirit to those who ask Him! (Luke 11:11-13)

Every good and every perfect gift is from above, and comes down from the Father of lights, with whom there is no variation or shadow of turning. (James 1:17)

Be anxious for nothing, but in everything by prayer and supplication, with thanksgiving, let your requests be made known to God: and the peace of God, which surpasses all understanding, will guard your hearts and minds through Christ Jesus. (Philippians 4:6-7)

Song recommendation: "He Wears a Crown" by Bryan McCleery

Conversation Starters

- Are you an introvert or an extrovert?

- Have you ever moved to a new city and had to start your life all over?

- Have you experienced the Law of Christ by sharing your troubles with a Christian brother or sister? Describe.

- How does worship change your heart toward God and others?

13 - What's Got Your Goat?

September 19 (Recalling Good Friday, April 19)

> "One has fear in front of a goat, in back of a mule,
> and on every side of a fool."
>
> E.W. Howe

Traditionally, Pastor Chris gives the Good Friday message. He has for all the years I've attended CrossBridge. This year, after the service, there was a huge block party in the parking lot — a celebration of new life in Jesus! It was with icy lemonade, sausage wraps, cotton candy, face painting, and even a petting zoo. The event drew an unexpectedly large crowd. Before the party, inside the church, it was standing room only, and oh so many kids.

Chris opened by saying he welcomed the noisy, fidgety energy. He told of a time of preaching in Nairobi, Kenya, when he'd invited people to come forward for prayer and a single wayward goat wandered down the aisle. Chris's lighthearted story and his relaxed demeanor calmed the people. He began to preach. He preached about Jesus' response to Thomas, his apostle, who is still known as "Doubting Thomas." In the end, Chris made a case for us to reconsider the label of this infamous apostle.

The apostle Thomas rightly earned that nickname. His doubt is undeniable. John 20:24-25 tells us, "Now Thomas, called the Twin, one of the twelve, was not with them when Jesus came. The other disciples therefore said to him, "We have seen the Lord." So he said to them, "Unless I see in His hands the print of the nails, and put my hand into His side, I will not believe."

Ouch. Thomas! Doubt much?

I am stuck in the mud of doubt, so I am thinking about Thomas on this September day. Not sure how I landed in the mud, and not sure how deep I'm stuck. I am doubting *everything*. Doubting my past self by rehashing past mistakes and doubting my future self by forecasting future mistakes. On Tuesday, my dad is having heart surgery, and I can't be in Pennsylvania with my mom and sisters in the waiting room.

In three weeks, my best friend is having her baby, and I can't be in Pennsylvania when she delivers. In one hour, my friends are meeting at Panera for brunch, and I can't even go across town to join them. My can't-be-there circumstances feel like muddy sludge in my heart.

I want to take a walk to clear my head, but I'm keeping a constant, watchful eye on Poppie Bob. We were sitting side by side on my back porch. He was staring blankly at a spinning suncatcher. I was silently simmering in my unsettled mood. Years ago, when Bob's mind was working correctly, he might have detected my disturbance and asked, "what's got your goat?"

And, suddenly, with that thought, I remembered the strolling African goat. I remembered the goats in the petting zoo at the block party. I remembered that I am not a goat. I am a sheep with a shepherd, and I know the *Good* Shepherd. Those memories galvanized me. I quietly snuck off the porch and dug around my office for my sermon notes like a little girl with a sand pail digging for a seashell. Devastated, I realized that I hadn't taken notes that *Good Friday* evening. I paused and prayed the muddiest prayer. The Holy Spirit generously enlightened my memory and rescued just before mud became quicksand.

Thomas doubted because he was focusing on himself. Ten of his comrades had come to tell him of seeing the Lord, and his focus was on what he would believe once he saw for himself. I related; minutes before my sermon note search, I was on the back porch, selfishly stewing in my own doubting mind.

I wonder why Thomas wasn't there when the other apostles first encountered Jesus. Did part of his *show-me-or-I-won't-believe-it* attitude stem from a bitter root of feeling left out? All the other disciples were there, and he wasn't. I can't add more to the story than what the Scripture records, but I know firsthand the callus that builds around the heart of someone who feels left out. I wonder if Thomas was angry with Jesus? How could Jesus show up and meet with everyone from the old gang except him? And the whole thing of life after death did seem a bit unbelievable.

When Thomas's fellow apostles come with their, "*we have seen the Lord*" testimony, maybe his doubt stemmed from his hurtful, confused, left-out position. It's likely that Thomas was rarely alone since he was called "the Twin." Perhaps *alone* made Thomas *vulnerable*, and vulnerable made him *uncomfortable* and in an effort to protect his heart, he cloaked himself with cynical *doubt*. Doubt is the germinating seed of unbelief. Thinking about that slippery slope unveiled truths in my own heart. I started to understand what had gotten my goat.

Thomas wasn't alone for too long. In just over a week's time, he rejoined his friend group. The Scripture tells us in John 20:26,

> And after eight days His disciplines were again inside, and Thomas with them. Jesus came, the doors being shut, and stood in the midst, and said, "Peace to you!"

I love that part: Jesus walking through shut doors and exclaiming the gift of peace. I also love the part about "Thomas with them." That helps me. *Alone* isn't a permanent state of being.

What Jesus did next is what I recalled as Chris's central message on *Good Friday*.

We continue in John 20:27, "Then He said to Thomas, "Reach your finger here, and look at My hands; and reach your hand here, and put it into My side. Do not be unbelieving, but believing."

Jesus knew of Thomas' doubt. He addressed it directly. That is clear. On the back porch again, sitting quietly next to Poppie, I thought about Jesus knowing my doubt.

Exactly five months ago, on that *Good Friday* night, Chris cautioned us to pay attention to the tone in which we hear the words from Jesus to Thomas. I hadn't thought about it before, but when I did, I admit, I was overlaying a tone of, at best, disappointment, and at worst, disgust.

Chris said that if we coated condemnation in those words of Jesus, we were not alone. He even suggested that perhaps the commonness toward imagining condemnation is *why* history has been so hard on poor old Thomas. It's almost as if to think, *Well if Jesus is scolding Thomas for his doubt, we should, too.*

However, Chris assured us that Jesus' tone would *not* have been harsh, scolding, and judgmental. Condemnation never fits with Jesus' character. Chris was insistent. He knew that to undo the thick layer of condemnation by our "inner critic," he would have to be emphatic in his challenge to us to hear correctly. Wow. I remember being astonished at how I had misheard those particular red-letter words. The church, jammed with hundreds of people, went silent. Everyone over the age of reason took in the much-needed certainty that Jesus words were spoken in a tone of love and gentleness.

Chris continued with reassurance: Jesus, the newly resurrected Christ, was inviting Thomas to erase his doubt with truth. Jesus met

Thomas exactly where he was. He met him with kindness. He met him in the middle of his doubt. The Solid Rock pulled His doubting disciple out of the mud pit. Jesus offered Thomas the chance to overcome by seeing, touching, and believing. And, true to form, Jesus gave appropriate "next step" instructions, "Do not be unbelieving, but believing."

The encounter Thomas had with the risen Lord melted away the dross of doubt. Scripture demonstrates a visible attitude adjustment: "And Thomas answered and said to Him, "My Lord and my God!" (v.28).

I asked Jesus to pierce my unraveling heart with his kindness, pull me out of the mud, and change my cynical attitude. I read the rest of the story. I focused on hearing with the correct tone of voice, which is the voice of love, without any trace of condemnation. My spirit strengthened.

> Jesus said to him, Thomas, because you have seen Me, you have believed. Blessed are those who have not seen and yet have believed." And truly Jesus did many other signs in the presence of His disciples, which are not written in this book; but these are written that you may believe that Jesus is the Christ, the Son of God, and that believing you may have life in His name. (v.29-30).

I remembered how Chris's sermon highlighted that last verse about having life in His name. He said there is a reason that the Friday before Easter Sunday is *Good,* and how every day after that day has been a good day for all believers everywhere and for all time. We were having the block party to rejoice over the death of our former sinful selves and the birth of our new-creation selves! The once-for-all sacrifice of Jesus meant freedom from the penalty of sin (death), and having life in Him was the best reason to celebrate.

Washing my mind with the truths spoken on April 19th fixed the emotional mudslide of September 19th. I felt joy well up in my soul. I longed to tell Poppie Bob about my goat of anger fleeing in the presence of the Spotless Lamb. Instead I just sat very still in a state of wonder, awe, and gratitude for the finished work of the cross of Jesus Christ.

Whatever became of the formerly doubtful Thomas? Chris told us that, according to historical records, Thomas went to India as a church planter and an evangelist, spreading the good news of the gospel. I bet his testimony was powerful. I bet he told people of Jesus as savior, how Jesus is the gate of righteousness. I bet he told people of Jesus as Lord, how Jesus has authority over all things. And, how could he not have told people of Jesus as life, the very fabric of our new life? I wonder if Thomas, traveling the many roads in India, told them of the prophetic words Jesus spoke to all of the disciples prior to His crucifixion, "A little while longer and the world will see Me no more, but you will see Me. Because I live, you will live also." (John 14:19).

Chris encouraged us to think about the transformation that an encounter with the resurrected Christ caused in Thomas' life. History has not been kind to Thomas. But, in reality, the powerful truth was that Doubting Thomas, in the end, was Believing Thomas, Evangelizing Thomas, Church-Planting Thomas. I have been thinking about that.

So, I took hold of the gentle encouragement Jesus gave to Thomas. I made it my own, "Do not be unbelieving, but believing." My insecurities and loneliness evaporate when I think about this. It's like soothing comfort to my soul.

Reflections & A Tune
Now if we died with Christ, we believe that we shall also live with Him, knowing that Christ, having been raised from the dead, dies no more. Death no longer has dominion over Him. For the death that He died, He died to sin once for all; but the life that He lives, He lives to God. (Romans 6:8-11)
In this you greatly rejoice, though now for a little while, if need be, you have been grieved by various trials, that the genuineness of your faith, being much more precious than gold that perishes, though it is tested by fire, may be found to praise, honor, and glory at the revelation of Jesus Christ, whom having not seen you love. Though now you do not see Him, yet believing, you rejoice with joy inexpressible and full of glory, receiving the end of your faith- the salvation of your souls. (1 Peter 1:6-9).
And as it is appointed for men to die once, but after that the judgment, so Christ was offered once to bear the sins of many. To those who eagerly wait for Him He will appear a second time, apart from sin, for salvation. (Hebrews 9:27-28).
Song recommendation: "O God Forgive Us" by For King & Country

Conversation Starters

- What is your most recent example of being left out? How did you feel? How did you handle it?

- In what ways do you struggle with doubt? What helps you overcome?

- When you picture God, do you ever see Him as angry and impatient with you? Give an example. How can you know for sure that He's not mad at you?

- Do you have a Good Friday service at your church? What are your church's traditions to celebrate the Passover?

14 - Quotable Quotes

Book Meeting, September 26

"Stronger than an army is a quotation whose time has come."
W.I.E. Gates

Barry and I both made appointments for four o'clock today. I scheduled to meet Chris, knowing Barry would be home from work in time to shower and then sit with Pops. Not noticing **"4:00 Book Meeting"** written in bold Sharpie ink on our family calendar, Barry scheduled a dentist appointment.

So, Chris met with me *and* Poppie today. We arrived early. Chris's office was arctic with air-conditioning. I got Poppie snug-as-a-bug in a cozy chair with a blanket tucked around his frail legs. The cold felt terrific to me: a welcome reprieve from the still-scorching south Texas heat.

Chris had been away from San Antonio for a few days last month to take Anna to start her *Link* year in Missouri. While he was gone, his staff spruced up his office. My eyes took in the new décor. Thankfully, they left several seashells. They added this cool display of nametag lanyards. It starts at the top of the office ceiling and comes down about seven feet: a waterfall of education, training, conferences, seminars, and retreats. Sixteen years' worth of ministry events cascaded down beautifully.

His staff left the wall on the right with the large whiteboard unaltered. It was strange to see the whiteboard without a thousand things written on it. On the side farthest from the door, the whiteboard contained a long to-do list. It felt like a breach of privacy to read what the tasks were, so I glanced away.

Chris arrived and greeted me. He met Bob, whose hands were occupied with his cup of juice and a cookie I had taken along for him. I took his cup so he could shake Chris's outstretched hand. Simple gestures like a proper greeting are so dignifying to the elderly. I savor them with and for Bob. Surprisingly, Bob remembered Chris from seeing him on Sunday through CrossBridge's live-stream service. Barry worked on Sunday so we watched from home.

We hadn't had a book meeting since July, so today was a catch-up session. We covered a lot of ground, talking about this and that and everything. Chris suggested a few editorial revisions to the text and proposed that we hunt down quotes to complement each chapter title. I have a book of quotes at home. I told him I would look through and then share with him. We talked about quotes for a minute.

Chris spoke about productivity in work and writing: how setting goals is necessary, how goals require contemplation and commitment. He mentioned Mark Twain and his prolific writing career. I mentioned John Steinbeck. He wrote *The Grapes of Wrath* in five months, 619 pages of a masterpiece in just *five* months. It had already been five months since our first book meeting in May. Emboldened by the mention of two literary giants, I ambitiously threw out a target completion date for our book. I blurted out, "December."

Chris brought me back to center by suggesting we ask God for direction. He said that he'd prayed about our book on his drive to our meeting. He let me in on one of his forms of prayer. He said that he'd read something recently that mentioned this prayer method as a way to clear away mental clutter and connect with God amidst competing distractions. He listens to worship music and then takes a lyrical line (or several), personalizes it, and prays. The song that got him praying on the drive over was called *Bigger Than I Thought*. I found it on YouTube and I'm listening to it now. It's a perfect prayer song. The line Chris prayed was that God was bigger than we think. In context, the song goes, "I throw all my cares before you. My doubts and fears don't scare you; you're bigger than I thought you were. So, I stop all negotiations with the God of all creation. You're bigger than I thought you were." Indeed, He is bigger than we think. I am thankful for Chris's automatic course correction with his wisdom to seek God's will for our book-writing deadlines.

Two days earlier, I was entertaining defeatist thoughts, and within minutes my phone chimed with a text from an old Army battle buddy. The text went to a group of us who worked at Walter Reed Army Medical Center in Washington, D.C. We are occupational therapists who worked together as a treatment team in trauma and amputation care. Harvey was texting us with a photograph of Uncle Vito and his soon-to-be published book. Uncle Vito is Vito Anthony and his new book is called *Americans, Don't Tread on Me*. I met Uncle Vito through a this-then-that series of happenings. Looking back, I see God's providential fingerprints. I told Chris about Uncle Vito, a Vietnam Veteran from Michigan, and the particulars of how we met in 2004, through an Op-Ed piece that ran in the *Detroit Free Press*.

We talked about a wounded warrior named Mario Lopez. He and his family attend CrossBridge. Mario wrote a captivating book called *How I Know — A Story to Strengthen Your Faith*. Aaliyah, Mario's daughter, attends Ablaze and is friends with Sarah Grace, Chris's youngest. I told Chris the Ernest Hemingway quote that epitomized my Army career of working with the catastrophically wounded: "The world breaks everyone and afterward many are strong at the broken places."

I'm sure Vito is *somebody's* uncle, but he's not mine or Harvey's or any other therapist's on the group chat. Vito became family. He earned his Uncle when he invested immeasurable resources of time and money in our mission of caring for military members wounded during Operation Iraqi Freedom and Operation Enduring Freedom (the Afghanistan campaign). Besides being a sweet reminder of good old days gone by and friendships that have stayed strong, the text from Harvey was a measure of reassurance that this book would also have a place in God's Kingdom, in His way, in His time, and for His people. With Chris's encouragement to work diligently and pray for God's direction on all deadlines, I heard an echo of Moses' psalm, "So teach us to number our days that we may gain a heart of wisdom." I quickly numbered the days until the very end of December. Ninety-six. I asked the Holy Spirit for Steinbeck-level fortitude.

I also told Chris about Robert Bateman, a naturalist and an incredible artist. He mostly paints in acrylics, and mostly animals and nature. I hope to one day buy a print for Barry entitled *Courtship Display*. It's of a wild turkey in a full-feather strut. Barry is a turkey hunter. When I was stationed in Kentucky, he volunteered for two years on the *National Wild Turkey Federation*. Bateman paints with such detail you look twice to see if you're viewing a photograph or a painting.

Bateman, now 86 years old, is still compelled to paint. I read a book about him; he said he would paint even if no one ever looked at or bought his paintings. Selling art is not his thing. *Making* art is his thing. Painting is his purpose. It seems that when we function from the very center of our God-given purpose, we lose the need for feedback or any form of attention, affirmation, or approval. When we focus on our purpose, favorable outcomes fall in place. And, ironically, dropping the need for feedback from anyone other than God seems to create a confidence that actually draws attention, affirmation, and approval from people. I like to be around people who are free to be who God called them to be. Too many times I foolishly focus on feedback. I thought up a quote about the serenity of feedback-free folks: "Purpose-pursuing people are not prone to be people-pleasers."

My Josh is a hobby artist — pencil and painting, but mostly pencil. He is like Bateman in that he is compelled to create things. He always was. I knew it when he drew a near-perfect circle at the age of two with his dominant left hand. Chris saw some of Josh's artwork in June when he, Ann Marie, and their girls came over with his Ablaze Summer Interns. Barry, William and I hosted a dinner for them at our house. Family dinners is one of the ways Chris introduces his Summer Interns to the body of believers at CrossBridge. One of Chris's interns was an artist so I got to showing off Josh's framed pieces scattered about the house.

Josh was recently on military leave from San Diego. He was home for a long weekend so we could take a family photograph with Poppie. We were recreating a photo that we had taken thirteen years ago. My heart could burst when I look back at how young the boys were in the first photograph.

During his time at home, over a huge home-cooked breakfast, Josh and I talked about Robert Bateman. I had a Bateman picture book on the living room coffee table for Poppie Bob to enjoy. Josh told me that writing was *my* purpose, and I had to do it, regardless of future book sales. His words reassured me. He reminded me of something I'd said long ago, but had forgotten. When I was in graduate school, I told my dad, who is a master woodworker and cabinet maker, that he was a *wood* carpenter and I was a *word* carpenter. I explained to him that I sanded down each sentence, crafted each paragraph with a chisel, and ultimately hammered out my dissertation.

Thoughts of creating things reminds me of a truth about our Creator found in Ephesians 2:10. It says that *we* are *God's* masterpiece, His handiwork, His craftsmanship. The Greek word is "poema." It's where we get our word, "poem." We are God's creation. He is sanding, shaping, and chiseling us. And, like a poem, He is writing the story of our lives. All of these thoughts make me think less and less about the eventual outcome of this book. The creative writing process is what is calling me. Perhaps the process is actually the purpose.

During our meeting, Chris and I also talked about his Sunday sermon. I gave him feedback from the flock. Sunday night, I'd attended my adult life group where one family in particular was quite touched. I'd also heard positive comments from last night's Ablaze life group. Chris shyly said what he always says to compliments, "Well, bless God!" He's like Bateman, that is, compelled to his purpose of preaching, and less interested in favorable feedback.

Chris preached on a Christ-centered cure to anxiety. In this *Age of Anxiety*, who doesn't need a fresh word of hope, and a strategy or two? Chris rightly said that believers come to church to get godly counsel to live better-equipped lives. He went on to say that the lost world will never be impressed if we sing about the Prince of Peace and then go out and live lives of anxiety, looking very much like the hurting world we are meant to be salt and light to. His message was full of truth and strong in power. I told Chris that I will write a chapter about it. I'd sent him an email later, thanking him for participating in the book project. Maybe readers *will* buy our book, I thought. Maybe readers will be strengthened by it, and encouraged to replicate the sheep-and-a-shepherd discipleship process. I will never paint a Bateman-like masterpiece, but maybe when I am 86 years old I will still be compelled to write sermon notes and dialogue with my pastor, continually answering the call to discipleship.

So, in the safe space of my shepherd-pastor-friend's newly decorated, freezing cold office, I galvanized my resolve to be steadfast in pursuit of my purpose to write the book that God gave me a vision of back in February. From start to finish, this was a very helpful book meeting.

Chris carried my purse and laptop bag, and helped me slowly walk Poppie to the van. Each of us held one of his knobby-knuckled hands, hands that had worked diligently and dexterously with electronics for over fifty years. When William and Josh were young, they would take apart electrical things (without asking!) and I often wondered if there was a genetic origin to their curiosity and capability. For as little time as my boys spent with Poppie, there were remarkable similarities.

On our drive home, I heard Chris Tomlin's song *Is He Worthy?* I tried Pastor Chris's prayer technique, praying that the glory of the Lord would be prominent in our midst for He *is* worthy of all blessing and honor and glory.

Walking into my house, I hung my bag and purse on the tall coat rack overcrowded with hats. I keep meaning to sort hats and clear the coat rack. Mark Twain's cautionary words against procrastination that stuck from graduate school flashed in my mind: "Continuous improvement is better than delayed perfection." I set my heart to heed Mr. Twain. When I got Poppie safely settled in his familiar spot on the back porch, I made quick work of revising the text according to Chris's comments, and I searched high and low until I found my book of quotations. As for the hats, I will sort them later.

Reflections & A Tune
For do I now persuade men, or God? Or do I seek to please men? For if I still pleased men, I would not be a bondservant of Christ." (Galatians 1:10)
"O LORD, You are the portion of my inheritance and my cup; You maintain my lot. The lines have fallen to me in pleasant places; Yes, I have a good inheritance. (Psalm 16:5-6)
Song recommendation: "God of All My Days" by Casting Crowns

Conversation Starters

- If you were to write a book, what would it be about?

- Would you let someone redecorate your office? If yes, who? And, why them?

- What is your favorite quote?

- Do you struggle with people-pleasing tendencies? How can knowing the Sacred Scripture help?

15 - Dead Chickens Can't Fly

> "No man knows how bad he is till he has tried very hard to be good."
>
> C.S. Lewis

Ablaze was wild. Chris's preaching was wild, *fantastically* wild. And, he had every wild teenager's attention. He had this large, uncooked chicken in a clear plastic bag. As he preached, he threw it up in the air and let it fall on the stage. Each toss in the air and thud onto the stage emphasized his point.

His point was simple: dead chickens can't fly.

He was teaching from the Apostle Paul's letter to the Romans. Chris is a *doctrine guy* and Romans is his favorite book in the Bible. His message was the finest explanation between law and grace I've ever heard, and in this case, *saw*.

The law is God's ultimate standard. It's a standard of perfection. Because of our sin nature, given to us through our inherited spiritual bloodline in Adam, we cannot meet the perfect standard of the law. Trying to meet perfection in our sin state is like that raw, dead chicken trying to fly. It can't be done. No amount of effort can make a dead chicken fly. Chris threw that chicken six or more feet into the air and stressed that in order to fly, that dead chicken must first be made alive.

The only hope for that dead chicken is to acknowledge his deadness and seek a new life and a new way to fly. That *new* way, that *new* life, is through faith in Jesus Christ. Jesus is the only perfect man who was able to fulfill the perfect law. Matthew 5:17-18 is Jesus assuring us, "Do not think that I came to destroy the Law or the Prophets. I did not come to destroy but to fulfill. For assuredly, I say to you, till heaven and earth pass away, one jot or one tittle will by no means pass from the law till all is fulfilled." In Romans, Paul writes it like this, "For Christ is the end of the law for righteousness to everyone who believes." (10:4). In other words, the law is still doing its job for all unbelievers (dead chickens) in the world, but to those who believe in Jesus, the law is fulfilled through Jesus.

I got worried that the bag was going to split open because that chicken was coming down hard on the stage. I left my seat and went to the church kitchen to get another plastic bag. I ran into Daniel, a young preacher-in-the-making who helps Chris with Ablaze. Daniel was having the same worry. We searched for a large plastic baggie and shared our excitement for how wild Chris was on stage, getting the students fired up with chicken-tossing. Daniel found the gallon-size baggies and handed me one.

I left the kitchen and headed down the aisle toward the stage, but changed my mind. A mesmerizing mood had settled over the crowd of teenagers. I felt a full-body awareness of it, and I couldn't disrupt that atmosphere as I approached the stage. I found my seat and sat back down, my fingers fiddling with the zip-lock mechanism of the plastic baggie. I sensed that some students were grasping the freedom of the gospel for the first time. I sensed that some long-time believers were getting new insights with fresh clarity. I sensed I was.

Chris was saying that there's no amount of self-help or recovery for the dead chicken. A new life must enter in. And with that new life entering, there must begin a new approach to life. This is a new strategy for living under a new system called grace. He read Romans 6:14, "For sin shall not have dominion over you, for you are not under law but under grace."

The truth of Galatians 2:16 says the same thing:

> ...knowing that a man is not justified by the works of the law but by faith in Jesus Christ, even we have believed in Christ Jesus, that we might be justified by faith in Christ and not by the works of the law; for by the works of the law no flesh shall be justified.

In a different letter, to a different audience, Paul wrote about the purpose of the law:

> But the Scripture has confined all under sin, that the promise by faith in Jesus Christ might be given to those who believe. But before faith came, we were kept under guard by the law, kept for the faith which would afterward be revealed. Therefore the law was our tutor to bring us to Christ, that we might be justified by faith. But after faith has come, we are no

longer under a tutor. For you are all sons of God through faith in Christ Jesus. (Galatians 3:22-26).

Our new life comes *from* Jesus' life. Chris was back in Romans:

Therefore we were buried with Him through baptism into death, that just as Christ was raised from the dead by the glory of the Father, even so we also should walk in newness of life. (6:4).

The dead chicken represents what the Bible calls "the flesh." It is the old nature and its ineffective operating system. The flesh is the sin-soaked system of strategies for getting ahead. This way of functioning in the flesh attempts to make us feel good about ourselves. It's a considerably convincing system. If we aren't careful, we can highly regard this system. We proudly say things like "he's a self-made man" and champion and celebrate people who work tirelessly and get ahead. Ironically, this system of living always falls flat, just like that lifeless chicken crashing on the stage and almost breaking the bag open and spilling chicken juices everywhere. (Thankfully, the bag remained intact.)

In the letter to the Ephesians, Paul writes about this operating system, calling it "the course of this world," and he explains who is behind the system: "the prince of the power of the air, the spirit who now works in the sons of disobedience." (2:2). Because I came to know and trust in Jesus in my twenties, I remember struggling and striving in life under the old system. I think of it every time I hear the Jeremy Camp song, *Dead Man Walking*. I was a dead girl walking, going nowhere fast. And, at times, I was considerably convinced that I had it all together. It just never stuck, though. Depending on my day-to-day circumstances, I would get angry and my countenance would fall.

Last year at Ablaze Chris preached truth from the Old Testament. He told us the head-scratching story of Cain and Abel, the first brothers. We see the manifestation of sibling rivalry resulting in murder. Clearly, these boys inherited the deadly virus of sin from their parents.

I remember Chris focusing on a warning that came back into my mind that night as he tossed the chicken high into the air. It is a warning, and an instruction, from God:

So the LORD said to Cain, "Why are you angry? And why has your countenance fallen? If you do well, will you not be accepted? And if you do not do well, sin lies at the door. And its desire is for you, but you should rule over it. (Genesis 4:6-7).

Cain was operating from a flesh-focused, me-centered position. Even to this day, our spiritual enemy wants us to operate from a *me*-centered position. God warned Cain that sin would be at the door and He instructed him to rule over it. In several Bible translations, the words used to describe sin at the door are *"crouching"* or *"lurking."* Makes me think of a bad guy lying in wait. In fact, the King James Bible translation does give *sin* a personal pronoun, saying, "thou shall rule over *him*." Sin, when understood as Satan, is the tempter who wants us to be self-made men and women. Sin, as understood as a collective evil operating system or principality, wants to dominate our thoughts through fear, worry, self-made power, and various lusts and desires.

What Chris was teaching from Romans was that we could draw the line in the spiritual sand and stop trying to go the way of Cain, that is, to do *well* so we could feel *well* so we could be *well* accepted. We *were* accepted and that acceptance came only through the life and work of Jesus. And, *well*, that is good news!

We could never be accepted on our own merit. We would never measure up. And once we were saved by grace through faith, we certainly had good works to do because God prepared them for us, but thankfully, we wouldn't need to gain our acceptance through them (Ephesians 2:8-10).

Sin would crouch or lurk or lie at the door, yes, but we could rule over it or him by faith in Jesus who eternally rules over all things, including sin (in all forms), and death. Chris put it like this, "Give up and look up!"

He quoted Romans 8:6-9:

> For to be carnally minded is death, but to be spiritually minded is life and peace. Because the carnal mind is enmity against God; for it is not subject to the law of God, nor indeed can be. So then, those who are in the flesh cannot please God. But you are not in the flesh but in the Spirit, if indeed the Spirit of God dwells in you.

That section of Scripture was the launch point for the Ablaze life group discussion. Oh my, did the young freshman girls ever need to grasp hold of the truth that the law of the Spirit of life in Christ Jesus had made them free from the law of sin and death (Romans 8:2-3). Through talking, they were realizing, and strengthening their confidence, that they no longer needed to be obsessed with their own efforts, their own sin struggles, their own self-righteousness. They were free from slavery to sin, and free from slavery to self. That freedom, in fact, had placed them under the management and rule of a loving King.

King Jesus ushers in His peace and joy. King Jesus offers power through His Holy Spirit. King Jesus gives rest from the hamster-wheel first spun by Eve's delinquent son Cain who wrongly thought that his futile effort could earn him approval. King Jesus invites us to work for Him, knowing that our heavenly treasure won't rust or be destroyed. He's guarding it!

That night, we left Ablaze knowing we were believers, pardoned from the penalty of sin, justified as holy and righteous, and made alive in Christ, transferred out of the kingdom of darkness and into the kingdom of light. I wanted Chris's saying on a bumper sticker, or maybe a new tattoo: *"Give up and look up!"*

We left Ablaze knowing that, though we still feel the forces of sin working in opposition against us, sin as an operating system no longer defines us, and we can freely and frequently say, "I now walk in the light as He is in the light."

We left Ablaze knowing that sin as an evil task-master no longer rules over us, and we can freely and frequently say, "Not today, Crouching Dragon! I am not your slave. I work for King Jesus now!"

We left Ablaze like born-again chickens, flying free.

Reflections & A Tune
For the wages of sin is death, but the gift of God is eternal life in Christ Jesus our Lord. (Romans 6:23)
Let no one deceive you with empty words, for because of these things, the wrath of God comes upon the sons of disobedience. Therefore do not be partakers with them. For you were once darkness, but now you are light in the Lord. Walk as children of light. (Ephesians 5:6-8)
Are you so foolish? Having begun in the Spirit, are you now being made perfect by the flesh? (Galatians 3:3)
For if you live according to the flesh you will die; but if by the Spirit you put to death the deeds of the body, you will live. For as many as are led by the Spirit of God, these are sons of God. For you did not receive the spirit of bondage again to fear, but you received the Spirit of adoption by whom we cry out, "Abba, Father." (Romans 8:13-15)
Song recommendation: "Dead Man Walking" by Jeremy Camp

Conversation Starters

- How have you struggled to accept the finished work of Jesus?

- How are you still keeping a spiritual scorecard? Are you ready to surrender that scorecard once and for all?

- In what ways have you been obsessed with your own efforts, your own sin struggles, and your own self-righteousness?

- In what life area or situation can you commit to the "give up and look up" mantra?

16 - Grief

Hospice Meeting, October 23

"You will be whole again, but you will never be the same.
Nor should you be the same, nor would you want to."
Elisabeth Kubler-Ross

Barry and I are on the first leg of our trip back home to San Antonio. We left Pittsburgh an hour ago and are headed to Houston. Last Tuesday, Poppie Bob took a turn for the worse and ended up in the hospital. His breathing was labored. He wouldn't eat or drink. He was weak. Barry had to practically carry him to his easy chair. We called our firefighter neighbor to help us get Bob to the van to drive him to the hospital.

It was a stroke. The doctor assured us there was nothing we could have done to prevent it. A chest X-ray also showed pneumonia. Did we miss something? He wasn't coughing and had not had a recent cold. We felt horrible, and our tears wouldn't stop. Bob was admitted to the hospital that night. Our friend from CrossBridge, Pat, came and sat with us. Pat is a retired nurse of forty years. She explained several things. Matters seemed dark.

The next day, we had a hospice meeting with Dr. Aziz, the attending physician, a gerontologist who would transfer Bob to an end-of-life care center in town. There was no curative treatment to offer. We knew, of course, that Bob's Alzheimer's was progressing, but he had been stable in other ways. Dr. Aziz was patient, slow and kind in his explanations. His sentiments echoed Pat's. Things didn't look good.

We were devastated. Our minds spun. The bottom dropped out of our hearts. We couldn't take in a full breath. We asked to just take him home for one more time to sit on the porch and enjoy the hibiscus flowers. Could he have one more time to sit out front and watch airplanes, drink one more glass of blue Gatorade, pet our dog one more time? Bob called him "Blackie" because he was black, and he couldn't remember his name. There would be no more *one more time*. The doctor was honest with us. Was this really happening?

The hospital workers were kind and loving: soft hearts working hard jobs. The nurse on the ward, Patty, gave hugs. She said, "comfort care is my specialty." Coffee. She had coffee. She gave reassurance for peace, saying that we would get through this together. On Wednesday, our CrossBridge family came to the hospital to pray with us. Text messages and voice mails rushed in. Barry's sisters and one brother-in-law flew down on Wednesday afternoon. Early Thursday morning, before we could grasp what was happening, Poppie Bob passed away. Just like that. He took his very last breath during the prayer from the hospital chaplain. I forgot tears could come out so fast. They did. Grief was disorienting at all levels.

Not even a week later, we are headed back to Texas. The funeral service was in Poppie's home church, St. Joseph's in Mt. Jewett, Pennsylvania. Barry's sister, Beth, and her youngest daughter, Chelsea, sang *His Eye is on the Sparrow*. Beth's husband, Jim, gave a poignant eulogy that included the gospel. Their eldest daughter, Kate, spoke on behalf of the six grandkids and two great-grands (Kate's two children). She recounted so many old and precious memories. All of us ladies wore small decorative hummingbird pins in honor of Pops. He loved to feed and watch the hummers. His late wife, Bonnie, loved them, so, after she'd died in 1995, watching them was a way he honored her.

Bob had served in the Army in Germany at the time of the Korean Conflict. Immediately following the funeral, just outside the church, in the plush green lawn, the local VFW did a flag ceremony and 21-gun salute. My eyes squinted into the bright mid-morning light. I held my salute during taps, tears flooding my cheeks. How many times had I done this while wearing my Army uniform? All stories of loss melded together in my heart. I was bombarded with memories of goodbyes. One big glob of grief overtook me. Each friend, coworker, or past patient I recalled losing was relevant, precious, and unique; each loss was personal, devastating, and distressing. Suddenly, I felt the truth of Romans 8, that the whole creation groans, eagerly waiting for the redemption of our bodies. The second to the last sentence of the Bible became my heart's cry: *"Even so, come. Lord Jesus!"*

Today, everything feels out of alignment. An emotional fog is heavy and obscuring my spiritual vision. And yet, I grieve with hope and promise of the eventual reunion of the saints. Tomorrow my praying friends from life group will show up and help me clean out Poppie's bedroom. I shoved all of his things in there before we left on Sunday for Pittsburgh. I hadn't realized how many of his things were in our main living area. Our home had become Bob's home, and our solitary task in life had become his care.

I took the shower seat out of our bathroom and moved it into his room. I wheeled his wheelchair from the entry way in there too. Bob called his spray deodorant his "do-good." It felt disrespectful to throw it away, and yet strange to save it. I took it off his cabinet and sprayed a little into the air and smiled. More tears fell. Here's a little splash of "do-good" for you, Poppie Bob. I wonder what heaven smells like. Cotton candy? Fresh bread? Apple pie? Fresh cut flowers? Barry picked up Pop's favorite white hat off our over-crowded hat rack. The hat said *FORGED* on it and was originally Josh's. Barry held it to his face in sorrow, breathing deeply, hoping for a familiar scent of his Pops' *Head & Shoulders* shampoo. I guess I never stopped to think about the many blessings of things that smell nice. I took the FORGED hat from his hands and placed it on Bob's pillow in his bedroom. I imagine it will always feel like his room, even when we are brave enough to turn it back into our computer room.

I moved most of Bob's things out of sight fairly quickly on Thursday evening, including the Robert Bateman art book. Barry went to the cupboard and saw Pops' half-eaten bag of Skinny Pop. The top shelf of the fridge held his half-drunk Gatorade. Frost blue, that was his favorite. Everything was a reminder of his absence. We parked ourselves down side by side on the loveseat, and just sat still together. The house was empty. We desperately wanted a distraction of something to do, and yet there was no energy left in our sleep-deprived, grief-stricken bodies. William had band practice and wouldn't be home until later that night, but we waited for his presence to fill us up.

I kept thinking of my Aunt Cheri, who had lost Uncle Bill earlier this year. I wanted to call her and say how much *more* I understood sorrow. I now felt how gripping, even paralyzing, sadness could be. When we left San Antonio on Sunday for the funeral, I wrote Cheri a long letter on the flight from Houston to Pittsburgh.

Surprisingly, this morning, before we left to reverse our trip and head back to Texas, Cheri showed up at my parents' house. She didn't mention my letter. I am sure it had not yet arrived in her mailbox. She had driven three hours, from her house in Chambersburg to Kane (my little hometown), because today would have been Uncle Bill's 63rd birthday. She was going out into the woods where his ashes were scattered. She would pray and think and walk and sit.

Aunt Cheri sat with Barry and me and my Mom in my parents' living room this morning. She held our hands and prayed that God's comfort would encompass us in this time of sadness. She assured us that Bob was in heaven, safe and sound, and we would meet again one day. She was a beacon of light. During her prayer, I thought of Jesus weeping at Lazarus' grave. Cheri came and wept with us. Even knowing the blessed assurance of eternal life, she honored our grief, and she wept. She entered into the sacred space of sorrow with us and through prayer she shone a light.

Barry admitted his eagerness for getting a head start on our drive to Pittsburgh, but Cheri told a quick story as she stood in the dining room getting ready to leave. She said that there are no coincidences in God's Kingdom. She told us that she walks every morning with her neighbor. They leave at 6:30 and walk three miles. They rarely miss, except for a time a few weeks back when the neighbor called and had to cancel because of an early morning doctor appointment. A few hours later the neighbor called and said she had a ten-minute window and wondered if Cheri was up for getting in a quick mile.

As the two ladies walked down their quiet country lane, a pick-up truck stopped and they had to walk around it. As Cheri walked behind the truck, she saw a red car and noted the driver, a young, college-aged man she recognized from her church. She popped her head down to the window to greet him. Sullenly, he pointed and asked about the corn field next to the road. Had it been cut yet, he wanted to know. No, not yet. Why? He seemed guarded and upset. She said, "What's wrong? Come out of that car and give me a hug." She hugged him, and he began to sob. He told her that his dog had recently died. He used to walk the dog in that field. He didn't know what to do with his grief so he skipped his college course and had driven out to the cornfield.

Weeks later, Cheri saw the young man at their church. He told her that the morning that he drove to the corn field he had prayed to God to send someone to talk to him and give him a hug. So, Cheri told us with confidence that there are no coincidences in God's Kingdom. God aligns things. A neighbor's doctor appointment allowed a missed morning walk to allow a later walk to allow a hug to comfort the grief that comes from losing a beloved pet. Cheri called these things "God-incidences." I want to remember that.

Barry and I wished Aunt Cheri a safe trip into the woods. She was boldly facing her grief with faith and hope. Her courage and strength sunk into my spirit. They are serving as an inspiration for me to type this chapter. Jesus includes His children in His kingdom work, that much I know.

Josh and William have a blessing in store. They bought Barry *Courtship Display,* the Robert Bateman turkey print. They are going to give it to him in the next few weeks when Josh comes home on leave from California. They will also all go into the woods and plant a tree in Poppie Bob's honor, drink blue Gatorade, and share some cookies. Poppie taught us *all* to share. Even in his last days, when his mind was all mixed up, if you gave him a single cookie, he would break it in two and say (or gesture because sometimes he had no words, only gestures), "Do you want half?" In his most confused state, he intuitively understood that when someone else was with him, he wasn't alone and anything he had was his to split in half and be shared.

I feel that splitting with grief this week. When someone shows up, and the burden is shared, the grief gets split in half. The memories of Poppie are already blessing me. I pray that as the emotional fog lifts, more reflections will come as little gifts: gifts of hope and gifts of light and gifts of love.

Reflections & A Tune
Precious in the sight of the LORD is the death of His saints. (Psalm 116:15)
Blessed are those who mourn, For they shall be comforted. (Matthew 5:4)
To everything there is a season. A time for every purpose under heaven; A time to be born, And a time to die. (Ecclesiastes 3:1-2a)
For I am persuaded that neither death nor life, nor angels nor principalities nor powers, nor things present nor things to come, nor height nor depth, nor any other created thing, shall be able to separate us from the love of God which is in Christ Jesus our Lord. (Romans 8:37-39)
Song recommendation: "Tell Your Heart to Beat Again" by Danny Gokey

Conversation Starters

- Have you lost a parent? What was that experience like for you? How did you mourn their passing?

- What is your most recent grief? How have you coped? Who has shown up and helped lighten your emotional burden?

- How does prayer meet a deep need during grief?

- What is the value of having someone who knows the pain of loss be present with you in grief?

17 - Zion

> "Man's course begins in a garden but it ends in a city."
> Alexander Maclaren

Tonight at Ablaze, Chris took us to the tower of Babel. He read the first verses of chapter 11 from Genesis: "Now the whole earth had one language and one speech. And it came to pass, as they journeyed from the east, that they found a plain in the land of Shinar, and they dwelt there. Then they said to one another, "Come, let us make bricks and bake them thoroughly." They had brick for stone, and they had asphalt for mortar. And they said, "Come, let us build ourselves a city, and a tower whose top is in the heavens; let us make a name for ourselves, lest we be scattered abroad over the face of the whole earth."

Chris highlighted the obvious: (1) there was one language on the earth; (2) the people were journeying from the east; and, (3) they found a plain in the land of Shinar and stopped there because they liked it and wanted to *stay* there.

And then, the less-than-obvious: first, language wasn't their only unity; they were also unified in a strategy. Three times there is a planning call to action: "let us." There are two statements of, "let us make," and one statement of, "let us build." There is evidence of their endeavor within the words, "Come, let us make" and "Come, let us build." Chris pointed out their self-reliance. They were intent on settling in the land they selected and were going to use their resources of stones and mortar to make a city and a tower for themselves.

The city would allow them to dwell together, and the tower would allow them to go up to, and perhaps they believed *into*, heaven. Either way, they were going higher. Planning, striving, building, establishing and climbing upward — these were their aspirations. Their unified language enhanced communication and allowed them to work well together. Man-made success was almost a sure bet.

On the surface, this doesn't seem terribly wrong. I recognize my own strong-willed nature in these ancient city planners and tower architects. Surely my interpretation is tainted by indoctrination in the American-dream culture where hard work and determination are championed. I am certain I would have bought into the idea of tower power, too. Let's build high: establish a vantage point for looking up, and looking out, and eventually looking down. I would have rolled up my sleeves, dug my hands deep into the mud, and started making bricks. I may have even sought promotion to leadership, demonstrating my ability to invite and inspire others by crying out, "Come, let us build! Come, let us make!"

So, what is going on here? Chris zeroed in on their motivation, which is revealed in the text, "let us make a name for ourselves, lest we be scattered abroad over the face of the whole earth." They had been named by God but instead wanted to make a name for *themselves*. It's not that they wanted to be famous in the modern way that we use the phrase, "make a name for yourself," but rather they wanted to be known for *their* strength, *their* ability, and *their* products. They formulated a plan to establish their identity based on the value of the bricks they made. They wanted to be the source of their own identity, thinking: *if we make excellent bricks, we will be known for our excellent brick work, and we will therefore be known for excellence, and therefore we must be excellent people.* The modern-day version of man-centered, materialistic illogic is the same. One of my own snags: *if I go to highly regarded universities and make highly regarded grades and get high-paying jobs and buy high-dollar items, I must be a high value person.* The all-too-common tangle is to make the *who* dependent upon the *do*. And, as Pastor Chris continued to unpack Genesis 11, I kept thinking of the 1983 movie starring Tom Cruise: *Risky Business.*

Chris continued. This was a people of God, instructed to be fruitful and multiply. They avoided God's command to go out and fill the earth. Instead, they settled in the plain in the land of Shinar, resisting the multiplying and the filling. Sadly, I didn't notice their rebellion until Chris pointed it out. And, after a closer look, I could see that they were a self-directed, self-centered, self-promoting people who, by focusing on themselves and their plans, were in opposition to God's plan and God's glory. Their sin was pride, and it was cloaked as ambition.

God made man in His image, which includes an inherent capacity to reason, plan, and accomplish incredible things. But, Adam and Eve desired to be *like* God and took Satan's bait to disobey God and eat the forbidden fruit of the off-limits tree. Sin entered the picture. Ever since, the intention of a man-centered heart is only evil continually (Genesis 6:5). It is subtle but it *is* certain: man, without God at the center, naturally becomes his *own* god.

But God sees straight through to the heart. And, what happened next is the cool part. Chris read the rest,

> But the LORD came down to see the city and the tower which the sons of men had built. And the LORD said, "Indeed the people are one and they all have one language, and this is what they begin to do; now nothing that they propose to do will be withheld from them. Come, let Us go down and there confuse their language, that they may not understand one another's speech." So the LORD scattered them abroad from there over the face of all the earth, and they ceased building the city. Therefore its name is called Babel, because there the LORD confused the language of all the earth; and from there the LORD scattered them abroad over the face of all the earth.

God gave them the capacity to achieve in their unity of language and plans, and yet He knew they were off azimuth. He saw completely, and He knew completely. He knew their plans were futile. And, like a good Father on a rescue mission, He came down. He loved them too much to allow them to stay in Shinar, united to establish themselves in rebellious self-importance.

The Ancient of Days, the One who knows the end from the beginning, perceived His people's blind spot and the error of their prideful hearts. He intervened. He came down. Chris said it several times, "God came down. God came down. God came down." Chris emphasized that God's gracious and good response to sin is to come down.

I had missed the miracle in the Babel story of God's coming down. I was focused on the part about God doing the confusing and scattering. I got the sense that most of us there at Ablaze that night had been equally puzzled over this passage of Scripture from Genesis. The Holy Spirit moved through Chris's preaching and shone light on God's wisdom.

In His perfect wisdom, God brought temporary confusion to bring the higher order — the intended order — in His perfect timing. God cannot accept a man-centered Plan B. His perfection will not, and *cannot*, accept sin. And, when I think about it, I wouldn't want Him to. God's thoughts and ways are higher than even my best and brightest thoughts and ways. Pride is sin, even when dressed up as ambition, hard work, and determination.

Chris told a story from his high school football days. His teammate, Jerry, caught the ball and ran eighty yards into the end zone. It was amazing! The crowd went wild with excitement and then immediately wild with frustration. A flag had been thrown for an off-sides penalty. *Chris* was the guilty off-sides wide receiver. While his entire team, their fans, and especially Chris wished the referee would have ignored the penalty, looked away from the error, and allowed the touchdown to count, ultimately no one wants to play with an unfair referee who looks over error and ignores the rules. Even a high school game of football demands a true standard of right and wrong. And, even the most desperate player knows the need for absolutes when it comes to fairness in judgment.

With his football analogy, Chris explained that God used confusion as a consequence of sin. Mankind was guilty of an off-sides penalty in Shinar and would only have been a slave to sin in the city of his own construction. When God throws a consequence flag, there's no challenge against His call. God knows that autonomy and independence are counterfeits to truth and freedom. So, God came down and confused their language for their ultimate good and for His name's sake.

A thousand or so years later, and fifty days after Jesus rose from the dead, God reversed the Babel curse. It was Pentecost, one of three Jewish festivals that involved a pilgrimage to Jerusalem.

We read about it in chapter two of the book of Acts.

> When the Day of Pentecost had fully come, they were all with one accord in one place. And suddenly there came a sound from heaven, as of a rushing mighty wind, and it filled the whole house where they were sitting. Then there appeared to them divided tongues, as of fire, and one sat upon each of them. And they were all filled with the Holy Spirit and began to speak with other tongues, as the Spirit gave them utterance. (v.1-4).

What a grandstand moment for the Holy Spirit. Diverse people from a variety of nations had gathered together in Jerusalem. The expected confusion of different languages was replaced by clarity of understanding through the Spirit's direct intervention to share the gospel with people in their native tongue. To this day, there are missionaries who, without formal training, are able to speak in other languages when sharing the good news of Jesus' coming down, and His life, burial, and resurrection.

I got home from Ablaze that night and was intrigued by Chris's preaching and what the girls had said during our reflection time in life group. I snuggled in bed and started reading Genesis from the beginning. I wondered all about the Garden of Eden and the Tree of Life. It all started there for us. I tried, but failed, to imagine the original innocence and freedom and purity and perfect communion with God.

When I hit chapter four, I was shocked by verses 16 and 17:

> Then Cain went out from the presence of the LORD and dwelt in the land of Nod on the east of Eden. And Cain knew his wife, and she conceived and bore Enoch. And he built a city, and called the name of the city after the name of his son— Enoch.

I stopped in my mental tracks. I was born and raised in a small Pennsylvania town named *Kane* so I have always found the biblical account of *Cain* interesting. And because of Chris's message, I now saw the obvious chain of Cain's sin. It was right there, an example of a five-step sin cycle:

Step 1. Cain <u>left</u> the presence of the Lord.
Step 2. Cain <u>dwelt</u> in a land east of Eden.
Step 3. Cain <u>made</u> his own family.
Step 4. Cain <u>built</u> a city.
Step 5. Cain <u>named</u> the city after his son.

I started to see how making a name for oneself emerges as a prideful, self-promoting strategy *after* leaving the presence of the Lord.

I woke the next morning thinking of Ablaze. One of my life group girls had asked a double-barreled question, something like, "Why does it seem like man still wants to build and make cities and live together in cities? Is it still a sin?" This was a sophisticated question for a fourteen-year old. It had me thinking. I asked William about it over breakfast. He reminded me of the coming Day when God builds the great City of David. William's middle name is David and apparently somewhere along the line he remembered that Jerusalem is also called the *City of David*.

Maybe wanting a city is part of our spiritual DNA, like a hidden longing. What God started in a garden ends in Zion. I asked William if he had time for me to read to him for our morning Bible study time. He was rushing to review his Calculus formulas for a test that day. He told me to read fast and loud. He toasted his chocolate waffles and packed his lunch. I quickly looked up a reference for the City of David on the Internet and then flipped to chapter twenty-one from the book of Revelation.

I cut right to the chase and read one chapter, the maximum daily dose for a seventeen-year old on the go. I read loud and fast. Here are three favorite sections:

Section 1:

> Now I saw a new heaven and a new earth, for the first heaven and the first earth had passed away. Also, there was no more sea. Then I, John, saw the holy city, New Jerusalem, coming down out of heaven from God, prepared as a bride adorned for her husband. And I heard a loud voice from heaven saying, "Behold, the tabernacle of God is with men, and He will dwell with them, and they shall be His people. God Himself will be with them and be their God." (Revelation 21:1-3).

Section 2:

> Then one of the seven angels who had the seven bowls filled with the seven last plagues came to me and talked with me, saying, "Come, I will show you the bride, the Lamb's wife." And he carried me away in the Spirit to a great and high mountain, and showed me the great city, the holy Jerusalem, descending out of heaven from God, having the glory of God. (Revelation 21:9-11).

Section 3:

> But I saw no temple in it, for the Lord God Almighty and the Lamb are its temple. The city had no need of the sun or of the moon to shine in it, for the glory of God illuminated it. The Lamb is its light. And the nations of those who are saved shall walk in its light, and the kings of the earth bring their glory and honor into it. Its gates shall not be shut at all by day (there shall be no night there). And they shall bring the glory and the honor of the nations into it. But there shall by no means enter it anything that defiles, or causes an abomination or a lie, but

only those who are written in the Lamb's Book of Life. (Revelation 21:22-27).

I prayed quickly over William before he left for school. "Stay in the Lord's presence and resist making a name for yourself!" He'd been at Ablaze last night and caught my drift. Standing on the stoop, I watched him drive away. He drives Josh's old car now. It's still strange to think of how fast Josh's high school years went by. I meant to tell William that God had named him His *child*, His *beloved*, and His *saint*. Why would any of us want any other names? I'll tell him when he comes back from school.

Off and on all day, I delighted in the fact that the desire for a city would one day be fulfilled. Satan would continue to tempt with a counterfeit, man-made city where God is pushed out, but God was at work building His kingdom. He was coming again to dwell among His people. What I felt that day was astonishment, and hopeful expectation.

Reflections & A Tune
Unless the LORD builds the house, They labor in vain who build it. (Psalm 127:1a)
I am the vine, you are the branches. He who abides in Me, and I in him, bears much fruit; for without Me you can do nothing. (John 15:5)
Therefore thus says the Lord God: "Behold, I lay in Zion a stone for a foundation, A tried stone, a precious cornerstone, a sure foundation; Whoever believes will not act hastily. Also I will make justice the measuring line, And righteousness the plummet; The hail will sweep away the refuge of lies, And the waters will overflow the hiding place. Your covenant with death will be annulled, And your agreement with Sheol will not stand. (Isaiah 28:16-18)
The LORD knows the thoughts of man, That they are futile. (Psalm 94:11)
Song recommendation: "God of This City" by Chris Tomlin

Conversation Starters

- What is your experience with self-will and (blind) determination? Give a life example.

- Has God ever thrown a penalty flag on your plans?

- What is your hope for the New City of Zion?

- Before you were born again (born from above, given a new spirit) you were dwelling in the proverbial city of your own making where sin reigned. Describe that time in your life and what the transition to accepting the Lordship of Jesus Christ was like? (Share your story!)

18 - Do I Have Your Attention?

> "You can understand why I am a believer.
> I have seen miracles."
>
> Dr. Ben Carson

Chris was a fifth-grader when his dad lost his job. He was unemployed for twelve months. Chris, his mom, his sister, and his three brothers worried in ways that kids and moms normally don't. The family's savings had been depleted. December rolled around. Christmas gifts were out of the question. The unspoken knowing of that settled heavy in their hearts.

Chris shared this at Ablaze. My spirit ached for ten-year old Chris. On December 22nd, there was a knock on their front door. His mom opened to greet a stranger, a stranger from town who had heard of their family's need. A stranger came to bring food and money for Christmas gifts. It was the Dillashaw's *"Great Christmas Miracle."* Chris's face lit up as he remembered.

Miracles leave us in awe. They make us wonder. They get our attention. Miracles aren't predictable, logical, or reproducible. And yet, they're verifiable. God may use people to usher in miracles, but the power and pageantry are otherworldly. Supernatural. Heavenly.

Chris told his miracle story during a sermon series through Exodus. He taught about God delivering His people out of Egypt. He taught about the ten plagues being God's displays of miraculous power over sin, slavery, and darkness. God multiplied His signs and wonders in Egypt so they would know He was the LORD. Moses told the Israelites that God heard their groaning, and He would redeem them with an outstretched arm and with great judgments.

The first nine plagues paved the way for the final one, The Passover, an invitation to declare allegiance to Yahweh by sacrificing a lamb and placing its blood on their houses' doorposts and lintels — a foreshadowing of the blood of Jesus placed in an array of the cross. God passed over each home covered by the blood of the lamb, and no death came to anyone in that home. God's message was, "Now the blood shall be a sign for you on the houses where you are. And when I see the blood, I will pass over you; and the plague shall not be on you to destroy you when I strike the land of Egypt." (Exodus 12: 12-13).

Chris showed an illustration of the plagues on the overhead screens. First, the water of the Nile River turned to blood for seven days. The fish died. The river stunk. This was a kick in the teeth to the Egyptians because The Nile was sacred to one of their idol gods (Osiris). It wasn't just the water in the Nile that turned to blood. It was *all* the waters of Egypt.

Next were frogs. Frogs were everywhere: in bedrooms, in ovens, in kneading troughs. I shuddered. When we lived in Maryland, we had a large frog in our house. Uncle Vito and his wife were in town to visit the wounded warriors. They were staying in our guest room. On the first night, we were sitting in our downstairs living room. Uncle V pointed, and said, "I think Josh or Will's pet frog got out of his cage." Barry and I exchanged a look. Neither of our boys *had* a pet frog. Embarrassed, we got busy capturing the slippery amphibian. Vito and Angel raised boys, so they were sympathetically amused. Given my experience of chasing out a single frog from my house, I tried to imagine an infestation of them in Egypt. The Egyptians worshipped "Heka," a frog-headed goddess. It was an offense to kill them. Sorry Heka, these frogs have to GO!

The third plague was itchy. God turned the dust of the ground into lice, which covered the Egyptian men and their animals. We've never had lice at our house, but both of my younger sisters' have had it in theirs. They washed everyone's hair with special chemicals. They shaved their sons' heads to U.S. Marine Corps standards. Their sheets and pillows and blankets and towels and clothes had to be washed with hot water and expensive soap. It was awful and time-consuming. When I was in the fourth grade, Mrs. Eckstrom made me and my classmates memorize the sing-songy rhyme, "Never share a hat or comb, or lice will make your head their home!"

An assault of swarming flies was the fourth plague. It got Pharaoh's attention. He promised to grant the Israelites freedom. But, after the flies were gone, he changed his mind and refused. Pharaoh's heart was prideful, and his actions were deceitful. God hardened his heart, like clay placed in a hot oven; the shape is the shape, and then heat firms or hardens it. In the end, the true nature or condition is revealed for what it was prior to the hardening effect of the heat.

The fifth plague brought death of the livestock. Their horses, donkeys, camels, cattle, sheep and goats became sick and died. Egyptians worshipped animals. Archaeologists have found mummified bulls. They particularly idolized black bulls. Imagine the Egyptians rethinking their veneration as their animal gods dropped like sick cows.

The sixth plague was boils. Moses and Aaron took furnace soot and tossed it into the air, which caused festering boils. The Egyptian priests were ousted from their temples because they had to be spotless.

Plague by plague, God was unraveling idol worship. Chris pointed out the specificity in which God got their attention, and the specificity in which God *still* gets people's attention. God works in *specific* ways based on the *specifics* of our lives with *specific* power at *specific* times. He is a personal God like that!

Exodus 9:13-35 describes the seventh plague. God would liberate His people. Justice would come in response to sin-driven oppressive slavery. Hail would be their attention getter. Isis, the Egyptian goddess of the air, would be dethroned. Innumerable ice balls would crash out of heaven and knock dents into things.

A few years back, San Antonio had an epic hailstorm. I stood on my front stoop in awe. Last Sunday after church, I was at Dunkin Donuts and saw a pock-marked car. I figured it had survived that hailstorm. It astonishes me how hail divots up a car.

As I listened to Chris preach, I thought about my fear of storms. When I was a fifth grader, my family's home was destroyed by a storm, a tornado, which is a rare occurrence in Pennsylvania. We lost everything. We moved to the other side of Kane until my parents could figure out what to do. I remember that first Christmas in our tiny rental. I remember what it is like to be ten years old, confused, and overwhelmed by worry. Having that experience is why I could feel for ten-year old Chris whose daddy was unemployed for a year. It's a particular grace when we can recognize in someone else's pain an echo of our own. Chris' humor pulled me out of my traumatic tornado trance.

He showed a scene from his favorite movie, *Princess Bride*, the 1987 cheesy adventure comedy. In the scene, the villain, Count Rugen, died in a swordfight with Inigo Montoya, who was avenging his father's death he had witnessed many years prior. After being seriously maimed, he regains his strength and focus, and says the iconic line, "Hello. My name is Inigo Montoya. You killed my father. Prepare to die." At the beginning of the scene, Count Rugen accuses Inigo with,

"Good heavens! Are you still trying to win? You've got an overdeveloped sense of vengeance," and then Inigo proceeds to inflict the same sword wounds to Rugen that he had received. This scene is appealing. We root for good over evil, for the oppressed to triumph over their oppressors, and for wrongs to be righted. Universally, we want the wicked to be punished. When the final blow is given to a villain, we cheer, "Finally!"

What were the Israelites feeling? They were safe and sound in the land of Goshen where not a single hail ball dropped. Did they hear the hailstorm? Did they see flashes of the fire that mingled with the hail? Maybe they cheered, "Finally!" Maybe they felt like Inigo Montoya. Maybe they said, "Hello. Our name is Israel. You ignored our Father. Prepare to die."

And, yet, prior to justice we see an offer of mercy! God told Moses to give the Egyptians a warning. "Therefore send now and gather your livestock and all that you have in the field, for the hail shall come down on every man and every animal which is found in the field and is not brought home; and they shall die." He who feared the word of the LORD among the servants of Pharaoh made his servants and his livestock flee to the houses. But he who did not regard the word of the LORD left his servants and his livestock in the field.

I opened to Exodus, this time with a highlighter. I highlighted mercy in the plagues. God issued warnings. Warnings are mercy. They are *good* and show *favor*. And, if warnings are heeded, they bring *good* and *favorable* outcomes. That's the point of mercy. Chris told a funny story about his two Labradors: the chocolate lab, *Piper,* and the yellow lab, *Baylor.* They love to eat. For the month of August, Chris didn't scoop their poop. It was August in South Texas, and it was blazing hot. He figured he was fine to let the piles pile up. Ann Marie was warning him. She was telling the truth that not facing the task would not make it go away. He did not heed her warning. Then one early September morning it rained. Actually, it poured all day long and well into the next day. Their backyard became a swamp. The rain stopped and the humidity skyrocketed to match the heat. And then it happened: Texas-sized flies descended on the doggie waste. Shovel in hand, Chris faced his dreaded backyard. The laughter of the students as Chris described his mini-plague was terrific!

Chris said, "Ask the deep questions of God! Don't put things off." I scribbled these notes,

> God is faithful.

God hears our cries.

He knows our hearts.

There's nothing God won't do to get our attention.

Prior to judgment, He provides warnings and mercies.

The warnings — mercy messages — from God through Moses to Pharaoh were stated similarly five out of ten times: Let My people go, that they may serve Me. But if you refuse to let them go, behold, I will...

God is not for genocide. We have Ezekiel 18:23, "Do I have any pleasure at all that the wicked should die?" says the Lord GOD, "and not that he should turn from his ways and live?" I thought about Rahab, the Canaanite woman, who declared her allegiance to Yahweh and was saved. I thought about Jonah calling his enemies to repentance. God issues warnings and lets each person choose to turn from their wicked ways and live. Proverbs 9:10 puts it famously as, "The fear of the LORD is the beginning of wisdom, And the knowledge of the Holy One is understanding."

The eighth plague was locusts: short-horned grasshoppers. There were so many of them that the ground was not visible. They devoured whatever countryside was left after the hailstorm. The locusts filled their houses. When we lived in Maryland we had several in our basement. Probably only three or four, at the max five, but it felt like a lot. They were only there for a single night. Barry was on an elk hunting trip to Colorado. Things go wrong, or seem worse, when he's not home. Around 3:00 am, I heard chirping in our basement. I tried to ignore it, but couldn't. I got out of bed, put on my bathrobe, and walked downstairs. As soon as I flipped on the light, their chirping stopped. One of them jumped. My heart jumped too. I noticed there was more than one. I got a fly swatter from upstairs and went back down to chase and swat them. I never even came close. Defeated, I went back to bed. The aerobics of chasing jumping locusts had taken away my sleepiness. Also, my mind was in overdrive wondering how they got in and fearing they would never get out. I lay there listening to the out-of-rhythm chirping, wondering if they were locusts or grasshoppers or crickets and what the difference even was. My alarm clock chirped at five o'clock. To this day, when I see the *Keebler Grasshoppers* in the cookie isle at the grocery store, I remember my strange night of locusts. I told this to Karlene, my friend in Massachusetts. She laughed and then nicknamed me "Katydid."

I have small personal reference points for frogs, lice, hail, and locusts, and I can even imagine the pain and urgency for relief from boils and swarming flies, but when it comes to the ninth plague, I have no context for a three-day darkness. The Scripture says this was a darkness that could be felt. No one could see or move about freely for three days.

The most challenging patient I took care of in my military days was a young soldier who had picked up unexploded ordinance in Iraq, and it exploded in his face. He didn't die. He almost died. He lost both arms and both eyes, but he survived. His lack of hands and his blindness kept me up at night. He still comes to mind. I know where he lives, and I get word on his status from colleagues; other therapists keep closer tabs. When Chris talked of the ninth plague, I thought of him. There is something unsettling about continual darkness. The idolatrous Egyptians took a blow with this plague because they worshipped the sun god, Ra. God turned off the sun (and moon) and gave them three days to think about Ra's lack of power.

When warnings aren't heeded, mercy is rejected and unbelieving hearts are hardened in rebellious form, and personal transformation is *not* possible. And from there, we understand why a just judge must *judge*. Exodus is a picture of God doing that. His ever-present mercies were rejected by the Egyptians. Their unbelieving hearts hardened. Transformation didn't occur.

Chris brought up a court case where a judge was lenient on a man guilty of murder. The town revolted. They wanted the hard-hearted murderer punished, not pardoned. We appreciate the predictable order of (a) choice (b) action (c) consequence. And when the choice is foolish and the action heinous, and no transformational response to mercy occurs, the penalizing consequence must be faced. Moses interceded for Pharaoh to bring God's mercy, but to no avail. Moses prayed on behalf of Pharaoh. That got my attention. The biblical record stands: Moses entreated the Lord to relieve the frogs, flies, hail, and locusts. That's four times out of ten a man of God prays for his enemy oppressor. And, God answered each of Moses' mercy requests.

Chris read 2 Peter 3:9, "The Lord is not slack concerning His promise, as some count slackness, but is longsuffering toward us, not willing that any should perish but that all should come to repentance." Chris challenged us to think of the mercy and justice of God and how they relate in perfect harmony. God never suspends one of His attributes to access another attribute. It's a mystery to us because we don't possess perfection in our attributes that way. Chris asked us to tune in to how God is moving in our lives, to let our hearts' attention be captured by God's mercy *and* justice. I pictured an old-fashioned radio dial in my inner spirit. I made a private idea with myself and tuned in to **FM** 100.7 for **F**ind **M**ercy 100% of the time, seven days a week.

After the sermon, our life group gathered upstairs in *Faith 45*: the fourth and fifth grade classroom. We split into small groups, so I was with just five girls. They had fun dreaming up modern-day plagues. They imagined God toppling the idols of social media, Hollywood, and the NFL. I smiled and assumed the girls' dads were consumed by football!

Lying in bed that night, I thought about the sermon and the girls' reflections during life group. I thanked God for His power to get people's attention. I thought of Chris's story of his family's Christmas miracle. I asked God to make me that stranger for someone in need this Christmas.

Reflections & A Tune
By faith Moses, when he became of age, refused to be called the son of Pharaoh's daughter, choosing rather to suffer affliction with the people of God than to enjoy the passing pleasures of sin, esteeming the reproach of Christ greater riches than the treasures in Egypt, for he looked to the reward. (Hebrews 11:25-26)
Who is so great as our God? You are the God who does wonders; You have declared Your strength among the peoples. (Psalm 77:13b-14)
I, even I, am the LORD, And besides Me there is no savior, I have declared and saved, I have proclaimed, And there was no foreign god among you; Therefore you are My witnesses," Says the LORD, "that I am God. Indeed before the day was, I am He; And there is no one who can deliver out of My hand; I work, and who will reverse it?" (Isaiah 43:11-13)
Do not let your heart envy sinners, But be zealous for the fear of the LORD all the day; For surely there is a hereafter, And your hope will not be cut off. (Proverbs 23:17)
Song Recommendation: "I Have This Hope" by Tenth Avenue North

Conversation Starters

- Has God ever gotten your attention with a miracle?

- Which one of the plagues fascinates you the most? Why that one?

- What idol would God need to topple in your life to get your attention? (social media, sports, shopping, food, career). Has He? What was your experience with the toppling?

- What do you think it would have been like to be Moses during the time of the Exodus?

19 - Tabernacles and Tears

"Tears are often the telescope by which men see far into heaven."
Henry Ward Beecher

Chris was preaching through Exodus. I glanced at the sixth graders; they're the youngest in Ablaze. They're small compared to the twelfth graders. Sometimes it startles me *how* small they are. They're like *"Ablaze Babies."* I considered the difference between the Sunday morning teaching of elementary school children and Chris' Wednesday night messages, particularly *this* message. Tonight, he was upgrading anyone's cartoon version of God.

I have no way of knowing, but I suspect that most youth pastors do not regularly preach from the book of Exodus. I was happy that there were so many Ablaze Babies present during this Old Testament series. I wish I could have heard about the Exodus when I was twelve. Chris definitely follows Paul's words of instruction in the book of Acts to preach the full counsel of God. I remember that segment of scripture where Paul says it because it's one of my favorite passages: Chapter 20. It has all the feels. I actually love the *entire* book of Acts because of the *Act*ion. It's my kind of writing: details, names, places, and plot.

During my two decades of military service, I heard many inspiring speeches by leaders, some with the high-brass rank and authority close to the President of the United States. None outclasses chapter 20 of Acts. After his speech, Paul knelt down and prayed with the apostles. They wept and hugged Paul before taking him to the outbound ship. They would never see him again. It's in that farewell address that Paul offers an encouragement to preach the whole counsel of God and to shepherd their flocks well as overseers, empowered by the Holy Spirit.

Before Chris preached his sermon from Exodus, he read Psalm 84. It's one powerful psalm. It's a psalm of places, as in places of shelter in the Lord's presence. It tells of tabernacles, tents, courts, alters, and houses.

There's a well-known declaration in verse 10, which was a key lyric of a popular worship song some years ago: "For a day in Your courts is better than a thousand. I would rather be a doorkeeper in the house of my God than dwell in the tents of wickedness."

Then Chris read Exodus 33. There are some real treasures there, and some mysteries, too. The LORD gave Moses bad news that His manifestation in the presence of their sin would mean their utter destruction, "...for I will not go up in your midst, lest I consume you on the way, for you are a stiff-necked people." (v.3)

God was still going to give them the land flowing with milk and honey, but He was not going to be their escort. God was going to assign an angel to guide them. God could not be near them because of their sin. That's a sobering thought.

As intercessor, Moses confronted his people and spoke the truth that God had revealed. I discern who a person *is* by what he or she *does*. I am limited to basing my thoughts and forming my opinions based on their outward actions. But God looks straight into the heart and knows who they actually are, and He knows who I am, too. Even if our actions deceive others, God can never be fooled, and the Israelites weren't fooling Him at all.

When Moses spoke the truth of their condition and God's decision to withdraw His presence, the Israelites responded correctly. They mourned. And, they stripped themselves of their ornaments. This was an outward gesture of humility and of hearts postured in sorrow over sin and a desire for God's presence. What they did next was another correct response.

Moses took a tent and pitched it outside the Israelites' camp. He called this tent the "tabernacle of meeting" and he sought the LORD. All people who pursued the LORD went to that tent. When Moses entered the tabernacle, the pillar of cloud descended and stood at the door and the LORD talked with Moses. The pillar of cloud was a sign that God was faithful to respond to prayer. Even when only Moses went to the tent, the Israelites saw the cloud and rose and worshipped by standing outside their own individual tent.

And in that tabernacle, Moses met with God. "So the LORD spoke to Moses face to face, as a man speaks to his friend" (v. 11). When I read that, I thought it meant that Moses looked full into the face of pre-incarnate Jesus. That is possible. I looked it up. It's called a "Christophony." But, later in chapter 33, it explains what was going on, and I realized that "face to face" was a figure of speech and means what the end of the verse says, "as a man speaks to his friend." I wonder what it was like for Moses inside that tent with the pillar of cloud hovering at the door.

After Ablaze, I read Exodus 33 a second time through, and I remembered how Moses was with Elijah and talking to Jesus when Jesus was transfigured in glory on the mountain where He had taken James, Peter, and John.

Peter spoke up and offered his service, "Lord, it is good for us to be here; if You wish, let us make here three tabernacles: one for You, one for Moses, and one for Elijah."

And guess what shows up? A cloud! Three of the gospels tell about this stunning event. A cloud overshadowed them. And God's voice comes out of the cloud, saying, "This is My beloved Son, in whom I am well pleased. Hear Him!" When Peter, James, and John heard God speak, they fell down afraid. Actually, they fell down on their faces, which is *all* the way and they were greatly afraid. A complete body, soul, and spirit experience! Jesus intervened. He touched them and said, "Arise, and do not be afraid." I pictured this scene. It makes sense why Peter would want to make tabernacles to contain the visible glory; and it makes sense how God speaking from the cloud would overwhelm to the point of falling in fear.

Chris told a story to get the students thinking about being near and having a healthy fear of power. At eight years old, he rode his bicycle everywhere. Pretending his bike had a motor, Chris dreamed of doing tricks and stunts like the famous Evel Knievel. One day his neighborhood friend, Dean, attached an old lawnmower engine to his bike and made a motorcycle. (I keep meaning to ask Chris if Dean's dad was involved in this engineering feat). Chris and the other neighborhood boys were impressed by Dean's new "motorcycle." Several days later, Dean let Chris try it out. With no way to handle the power, Chris took off full throttle: up a driveway, between two houses, through a rose bush, and through a fence that propelled him off the bike. He shot through the air like a rocket. Having escaped serious harm, Chris steered clear of motorcycles until college, and to this day he holds a keen awareness and respect for their power. Chris can take a boyhood memory and construct an allegory for reverence and allure to the might and majesty of God. The Ablaze Babies were laughing and caught his drift. Perhaps some were wondering how to get access to a lawnmower engine and attach it to their bikes. My sweet life group girls were asking if Pastor Chris broke any of his eight-year old bones!

Chris continued preaching. He zeroed in on the second half of verse 11 in Exodus 33, where Moses returned to the Israelites' camp, but his servant, Joshua, would not depart from the tabernacle. He asked us to consider the devotion in the example of young Joshua. Chris told the students that Satan would love for them to believe that devotion and worship are for old people. He said that our adversary, the devil, is working to distract us so we forget that God is within us, dwelling in us through His Holy Spirit.

We no longer need a tent of meeting to enter into God's presence. Jesus was God entering *our* presence. Trusting in Jesus' life, death, burial and resurrection as payment for our sins means we are the new tabernacle. Jesus paid the price for our sins. He gave us His Spirit as a down payment promise of our spiritual birthright to glory. A down payment is important, like when you buy a house and have to give earnest money to prove you're going to the bank to come back and claim full possession of the house.

Ephesians 1:13 and 14 puts it clearly:

> In Him you also trusted, after you heard the word of truth, the gospel of your salvation; in whom also, having believed, you were sealed with the Holy Spirit of promise, who is the guarantee of our inheritance until the redemption of the purchased possession, to the praise of His glory.

We also have the truth of 1 Corinthians 6:19-20 in the form of a rhetorical question from Paul and then a helpful instruction:

> Or do you not know that your body is the temple of the Holy Spirit who is in you, whom you have from God, and you are not your own? For you were bought at a price; therefore glorify God in your body and in your spirit, which are God's.

Chris was teaching many things to all of us: the Ablaze Babies, the older students, and life group leaders. He told us about being a middle schooler and getting an overwhelming, unmistakable call on his life to become a pastor. His adolescent heart was pounding. His faith expanded inside him. He seemed too young, and yet God birthed in him a desire for a life in ministry. Fast forward several months from that moment, and Chris' youth pastor asked him to close the church service on a Sunday night. Ten minutes. Chris had ten minutes to share a message. He skipped school on Friday to prepare.

Forty-something year old Chris described his first ten minutes of preaching to us that night. His motorcycle story had us all laughing and now with this story we were all sympathizing. With shaky hands and weak legs, eighth-grade Chris walked on stage, looked out at all the people and let forth a stream of tears. His message was ugly cries, nothing intelligible, just tears and feelings and a middle school body overwhelmed by emotions. Some of my life group girls were audibly supportive. I could hear them with their aahhhs and oohhhs.

Chris recalled something surprising following his first tearful sermon: he touched a lot of lives. After he walked off the stage, he got an incredible response from everyone. He felt embarrassed for his tears but they felt his heart. They connected with his honesty. Their own tears fell in response to his. It was powerful to just witness Chris' explanation of this; I can hardly imagine my response had I been there to witness it firsthand. Chris, actual grown-up bona fide *Pastor* Chris, spent the final ten minutes of his preaching that night encouraging the students to make conscious contact with God through the indwelling Holy Spirit. God is with each of us as He promised to never leave us nor forsake us. Talk about direct access to the presence of God when we are the temple of His Holy Spirit: no more tents, and no more tabernacles.

Chris said to start right where we were, that even the weakest faith in our strong God was a mighty force in the Kingdom. Chris suggested the young students discipline themselves, like Moses' servant Joshua, to be dedicated to God through prayer. Time spent with God reveals His perfection in every attribute, which increases our awe of His glory and power. This sermon inspired me to throw off my ornaments, get into that "tabernacle of meeting" inside my heart, open up, shed some honest tears, and speak to God face to face, as a man speaks to a friend. When I got into that interior, honest place, I felt the truth of Psalm 84 and knew deep down in my soul how much better is one day in God's presence than a thousand elsewhere.

Reflections & A Tune
You number my wanderings;   Put my tears into Your bottle; Are they not in Your book?   When I cry out to You, Then my enemies will turn back;   This I know, because God is for me. (Psalm 56:8-9)
But Christ came as High Priest of the good things to come, with the greater and more perfect tabernacle not made with hands, that is, not of this creation. Not with the blood of goats and calves, but with His own blood He entered the Most Holy Place once for all, having obtained eternal redemption. (Hebrews 9:11-12)
Thus says the LORD: "Refrain your voice from weeping,   And your eyes from tears;   For your work shall be rewarded, says the LORD,   And they shall come back from the land of the enemy."   (Jeremiah 31:16)
Now He who establishes us with you in Christ and has anointed us is God, who also has sealed us and given us the Spirit in our hearts as a guarantee. (2 Corinthians 1:21-22)
Song recommendation: "How Can It Be?" by Lauren Daigle

Conversation Starters

- God never leaves us, He is always accessible. How, then, do you make conscious contact with Him? (examples: worship, prayer, meditation, fellowship, a nature walk, observing a sunset).

- What does it mean to you to be "sealed with the Holy Spirit?" How is this good news?

- When is the last time you cried in front of others? What were the circumstances? What was their response? Did you feel better after crying?

- What does it mean to you to "live from the heart?"

20 - That's the Way the Cookie Crumbles

Book Meeting, December 19

"It is only with the heart that one can see rightly; what is
essential is invisible to the eye."
Antoine de Saint-Exupery

Chris and I met for our final book meeting. Well, it was scheduled as our final meeting, except that we ended up meeting one more time: a final *final* meeting. I am glad we met again. I loved the book meetings, the sitting and talking and listening and working together.

Growing up, I had several jobs. I babysat, cleaned houses, and worked as a cashier at the Quality Markets. The job I held the longest was delivering newspapers. I was eight years old, an ambitious third grader with a paper route. When I called my parents to fact check this, my mom jokingly asked if I was filing a law suit against them for violating child labor laws. We had a good laugh! I'm quite sure I insisted on working at such a young age.

When I was in seventh grade, I took over my older sister Karen's paper route, which was a really good gig delivering to *The Central Towers*. I added almost forty-five new customers to my original route by just adding that *one* building. My next younger sister, Kristen (a sixth grader), shared the now-joined paper routes with me. After school we walked together to Vincie's, a small Mom & Pop convenience store, to pick up our stack of newspapers.

We counted and split the papers, tucked them into our single-strapped, cloth newspaper bags, and then raced across the street and through the six floors of *The Central Towers*, dropping and kicking the papers under customers' doors. It was a great gig, and we were fast!

We still delivered to our original customers who lived in regular houses. Their deliveries took much longer. Plus, December through March each year, we had to wear snow boots and trudge through the piles to reach people's front doors. Our mom slipped empty bread bags over our feet to keep them dry inside our cheap winter boots.

Friday was our hardest paper-delivery day, because it was collection day. It took almost double the time and double the effort. It cost $1.25 for a week's subscription to *The Kane Republican*. We knew all our customers. For the interesting ones, we made up stories to fill in the blanks about what we didn't know. It became a game. Each house held a family, and each family held a story. To this day, Krissy and I share a nickname back and forth of "Derm," because of our near-perfect impersonation of Mrs. McDermott. She lived in an extravagant house near Vincie's. Mrs. McDermott had a matching extravagant personality. When I finished graduate school, Kristen gave me an engraved frame that read, "Doctor Derm." Some childhood memories stay strong despite the typical fade of time.

Kristen made a special friendship with Rosie Bonadio, an Italian woman in her eighties, barely five feet tall. Rosie sat in her wheelchair inside her little apartment at *The Central Towers*. She listened to an FM radio. Rosie loved music. She also loved for Krissy to sit with her and share stories. In turn, Kristen loved Rosie. I knew that was true because Krissy rarely sat still. She was packed with springs like a kangaroo. Sitting still took lots of control. And finding that control took even *more* control. While they visited, I ran my own kangaroo self to our grandparents' house just over the hill and across the railroad tracks. When I got to Grammie's candy dish, I took a few extra orange gumdrops. If Kris and I showed up together, she would oversee things with, "Why, you two share and see that you only take two pieces each." I suppose when you raise ten children, you never stop refereeing for fairness. Our dad is the oldest of those ten, and he's more kangaroo than Krissy and me combined.

Kristen would tell Rosie things that happened at school. If there was a bad ending (someone getting in trouble) Rosie would sigh and smile and say, "well, that's the way the cookie crumbles." Rosie never seemed troubled. She accepted life on life's terms. Her eyes sparkled even when her brow was furrowed trying to understand why so-and-so-middle-schooler would do something silly or foolish or even downright dangerous.

Rosie asked questions. Curiosity was her special gift; she inquired about things and people and ideas and what was going on over at Vincie's that day. Filling in the gaps of the story, Kristen and I said that Rosie and Vincie were boyfriend and girlfriend. They were about the same age. Rosie's false teeth clinked together when she said, "that's the way the cookie crumbles." Krissy used to imitate Rosie saying that. I went with Kris to visit Rosie on Fridays so I could hear for myself. I doubt we fully understood the *such is life* meaning of the idiom, but we certainly visualized the misfortune of a cookie crumbling.

After Rosie gave us her dollar and quarter, we would sit and talk. I told Rosie about Drew, the brown-eyed Italian boy at school. I liked him. He ignored me half the time and teased me the other half. Turned out that Drew liked my best friend Tosha. She had bright yellow hair and was allowed to wear eye-liner. Grammie called her a fashion plate. Drew was taking Tosha to the Snow Ball Dance. Unburdening my heart, I told Rosie everything. Her stillness and affirming presence made me feel safe. Sure enough, Rosie looked me straight in the eye (hers twinkling), nodded her white curly-haired head, and said, "that's the way the cookie crumbles." I felt better for having put words around the drama of the me-Drew-Tosha triangle. Kristen was more interested to know, "Did you hear it?" Yes, I heard it. I thought that maybe when they're not your own teeth, you're clumsier, and they clunk. That's what I told Kristen. She believed me.

Old folks sit still, look you in the eye, and listen. They have lots of time to practice so they get good at it. Rosie was in a wheelchair, so she had extra training. She didn't worry about what Krissy or I thought of her. She was too busy thinking about us. That made her genuinely interested in *our* stories.

Chris reminded me of Rosie. Not the wheelchair or false teeth, just the sitting still with curiosity running strong. Pastors are like the elderly. Or perhaps the elderly are like pastors. They sit still, offer their bright eyes, wise hearts, and undivided attention to each crumbling-cookie story.

During each of our book meetings, Chris sat, listened, and spoke with curiosity about people and things and ideas. Today he was reflecting on his work as a pastor and thinking about church culture in America. He suspected that by the time folks buckle their seatbelts and exit the church parking lot, many have already forgotten the sermon. They turn on their car radios and then chatter about what restaurant to go to for lunch and what time football starts.

Had Chris been an engineer, he would have had the advantage of seeing results of his work in the physical realm. Engineers, he continued saying, work from and toward straight angles, squares, and plumb lines. Feedback comes from positive *and* negative results and engineers can modify their efforts based on perceivable data. Chris talked about the differences between an engineer and a pastor. I understood what he was saying. I kept nodding. He was on to something. And then, Chris spotted a shining similarity with his work and the engineer's: offering order in exchange for chaos. And there it was, a glimmer of a shared purpose between the otherwise divergent careers. Being an engineer and being a pastor were linked in their purpose of creating order out of chaos.

I thought about carpentry and how it's like engineering. I thought about Jesus, the carpenter. It is an unmistakable wink from God to send Jesus, the Creator of the Universe, in human likeness to practice the trade of carpentry. Likely Jesus would have first submitted to his dad, Joseph's teaching and training. He would have been Joseph's apprentice. That makes me smile. Jesus: the original "Undercover Boss."

Jesus, humbly worked with His hands, creating, and building and likely, as all carpenters do, *re*building and repairing broken things. Profoundly and providentially, Jesus' earthly vocation as a carpenter represented what He was doing in the invisible, eternal world. Talk about exchanging chaos for order! Talk about a perfect plumb line!

I imagined Jesus talking to a potential customer, "Well, the demolition work here will be extensive, but yes, with your permission, I can rebuild your house. This current ground seems a little sandy, and I foresee some storms and high winds coming your way. May I suggest moving to more solid ground?"

"And how much is this demo, relocation, and rebuild going to cost me?" the customer would ask.

"Not a single denarius. I will do it as a free gift to you. Do you believe in Me? Do you believe that I can do this work?" would come Jesus' reply.

Chris has long understood that his work happens on life's unseen platform. But every now and again, engineer envy manifests. I understand that longing to see and know what reconstruction work is happening on the inside. I think every parent or teacher reaches a similar reflection point when the desire emerges to know if what you're doing is *actually* working and if you're building something that will last. Seeing the interior scaffold of godly character taking shape requires spiritual eyes. The construction of that scaffold takes a parent and pastor partnership. Hopefully, that pastor is like Chris, willing to work diligently, building sermon by sermon, week after week. Pastoring requires commitment to the long haul. Pastoring is like a Friday newspaper collection day in a blizzard with no bread bags on your freezing feet. You have to stick it out and receive encouragement when offered. Perhaps you meet a Rosie Bonadio in a cozy, high rise tower and get to sit still and clear your thoughts.

Chris smiled, stroked his goatee, and told me about a particular sermon many years ago. He'd spent hours preparing. He preached it to the entire congregation on a crowded Sunday morning. His message was on keeping an eternal perspective, not attaching and clinging to the material world because it could (and *would* eventually) disappear. True to form, he included an object lesson. He told of getting a new cell phone and failing to transfer over his contacts. He said how, just like that, all he had accumulated was no longer available and there was no way to recreate what was lost.

After the church service, Chris was mingling. A man saw him and made a quick approach. Chris was excited, anticipating that perhaps his sermon had greatly touched this man's heart. Pastors know that there may be two hundred people in the room, but maybe the message is going to transform only *one* of them. Instead, the man was eager to offer a tip to Chris about a new software application to download that would prevent unintended loss of data. Chris smiled and kindly thanked the gentleman for the tip. Inside, he sighed.

Some people are blind to the unseen, eternal world and when you include a parable in your sermon, they do not understand. I thought of Jesus crying out, "He who has ears to hear, let him hear!" (Luke 8:8). Chris admitted that working as a pastor without visible feedback of results is not for the faint of heart. I saw Jesus' heart reflected in Chris' honesty. It made me understand why Jesus would cry out his plea for people to tune in and listen. Good pastors, like the Good Shepherd, want all to come to a saving knowledge of God's grace through Jesus Christ.

I remember being a blind, lost sheep. Through the persistent prodding of a retired Army Warrant Officer who had traveled as a Christian missionary throughout all of Italy, I heard the voice of the Good Shepherd calling me. That retired soldier was Robert Nebeker. He was in his sixties and had undergone surgery. I cared for him at Evans Army Community Hospital on Fort Carson in Colorado.

At the time, I had a proper religious life. I was a morally good person. I wasn't as good as many but certainly better than most. And, I had added seventeen years of momentum to my paper route work ethic. I planned to present that as my spiritual resume when I stood at Heaven's gate. To me, Jesus was a one-dimensional character in the

Christmas and Easter stories, not to mention that in my church He still hung dead on a cross behind an altar. Plus, most of the time I was actually praying to His mother. Jesus was busy with other things, the church officials said. I had never heard the actual gospel. One time, as a high schooler, I'd read something about the idea of being born again. I scoffed! I reasoned that was a bit excessive, if not impossible.

Thankfully, in the year 2000, God sent Mr. Nebeker, a former Warrant Officer (military weapons expert) and a well-traveled missionary, to intersect my misguided beliefs and prideful attachment to them. He met me right where I was, stumbling on and offended by the very Cornerstone of Zion.

Through Robert's gentle demeanor, curiosity of my story, and presentation of the truth, I read the gospel of John. My twenty-five-year old eyes were opened, and I entered into Jesus' sheepfold, through His gate (He is the gate!), and exchanged my religious chaos for His perfect spiritual order. Robert guided me when I was just a "babe in Christ" desiring that pure spiritual milk of the word. I attended a Navigators Bible study and read the Bible with a ferocious appetite. I had a lot to learn. I had a lot to *unlearn*.

Barry, Joshua, and I moved away from Colorado. Robert sent us letters with extensive passages of Scripture copied in his exceptional handwriting. Come to think of it, each letter was like a book meeting tucked in an envelope. His messages differed, but they all conveyed that he had time for us.

Despite Robert's declining health, he emailed me faithfully throughout my military deployment. Sitting still in a bunker in the middle of the night in Afghanistan, I thought about God sending him into my life. In the January coldness, in that bunker, I remembered just how stubbornly I'd played the top-ram as Robert's therapist (as if the healing I was giving was the better offer), and there was Robert, shepherding me to the Good Shepherd who would exchange my dead spirit for rebirth to eternal life. His was, by far, the better offer. Gratitude overtook me and warmed me in that cement block bunker. To this day, I remain thankful for Jesus' love, His calling, for Robert's obedience (and boldness), and for our common salvation.

Robert introduced me to Jesus, the carpenter, the engineer of eternity, the One who no longer hangs on a cross, who definitely does not want me to pray to His (earthly) mother. I met Jesus, the one who demolished my religious strongholds and relocated and rebuilt my life on His perfect, finished work. No more altars. Jesus was the once-for-all, one-time, perfect sacrificial lamb.

I am also thankful for the long-haul work of pastors, chaplains, and Christian brothers and sisters. Year in and year out, whether by letter, email, or sermon, faithful and dedicated people built my inner spiritual scaffold. It's some of the best engineering and carpentry work. Invisible, *yes*, but eternal.

One day, months after returning from Afghanistan, I received a notification from Robert's daughter that he had died. I look forward to the reunion of the saints. It's powerful to have reassurance that Robert will be there. Hopefully, Rosie Bonadio will be too, using her new teeth to enjoy cookies that will never crumble.

Reflections & A Tune
He is like a man building a house, who dug deep and laid the foundation on the rock. And when the flood arose, the stream beat vehemently against that house, and could not shake it, for it was founded on the rock. (Luke 6:48)
Is this not the carpenter, the Son of Mary, and brother of James, Joses, Judas, and Simon? And are not His sisters here with us?" So they were offended at Him. (Mark 6:3)
For by Him all things were created that are in heaven and that are on earth, visible and invisible, whether thrones or dominions or principalities or powers. All things were created through Him and for Him. (Colossians 1:16)
Now, therefore, you are no longer strangers and foreigners, but fellow citizens with the saints and members of the household of God, having been built on the foundation of the apostles and prophets, Christ Jesus Himself being the chief cornerstone, in whom the whole building, being fitted together, grows into a holy temple in the Lord, in whom you are also being built together for a dwelling place of God in the Spirit. (Ephesians 2:19-22)
Unless the LORD builds the house, They labor in vain who build it. (Psalm 127:1)
Song recommendation: "Changed" by Jordan Feliz

Conversation Starters

- Who is the oldest person you know?

- Does he or she have any clever sayings that are frequently repeated?

- What was your first job in life?

- Do you have siblings?

- Do you remember your own story of coming to a saving faith in Jesus? Tell your story?

21 - Little Flock

"Nicknames are fond names.
We do not give them to people we dislike."
Edna Ferber

On a Sunday in September, Chris preached on overcoming anxiety. Five months later, I'm sitting in a soft-backed, yellow chair in my office, sorting through a stack of old papers and mail. Things pile up over time. Remember my little tree Calipari? It has shot up six inches since last year; its light green leaves look beautiful in the sunlight coming in through the large office window. Fruit flies are buzzing around, probably flew in from the kitchen. I need to make banana bread or toss the near-rotten fruit. Is today a baking day? I really should straighten up my desk first. I am indecisive. I am also anxious, which is why I was trying to clean up my office: trying to make order out of disorder to calm my mind down.

That Sunday back in September, Chris had preached to the *big* kids (adults) in the main auditorium. I wanted to be there, but I couldn't. Poppie Bob was having a rough morning: the kind of morning that told me it would be lunchtime before he was out of bed, washed, shaved, dressed and ready for breakfast. I distinctly remember the morning. Attending church was out of the question. My lowly circumstances of caretaking were out of alignment with my lofty expectations of socializing. As an idealist, I get caught in that gap between *lowly* and *lofty*. It's an emotional gap, a breeding ground for anxiety. It's scary and cold and lonely in that gap. There are fruit and pesky fruit flies galore.

My sermon notes were in a small, green journal which was under a pile of Christmas card envelopes I saved to update my address book. Military friends move a lot. As I read my journal, strong memories surfaced. I remember sitting at the kitchen counter with Poppie (unshaven, still in pajamas, teeth not yet brushed) watching the live cast of the eleven o'clock (second) church service. I remember him tapping my journal, *"Writin' a book?"* Tears rush to my eyes as I think of that now.

Normally I have a nice cursive style, but these notes were a messy print-cursive hybrid with fluctuating letter sizes. My handwriting was terrible. I switched pens half way through because the pen had run out of ink. I remember wanting to find another *blue* ink pen, but settling for the black one from a basket within reach right behind the barstool where Poppie sat. My sermon notes were literally black and blue. Symbolic. Handwriting analysts would detect the bruising of indecision, disappointment, and anxiety.

I remember Chris slowly and deliberately reading Luke 12: 22-32. The entire segment is Jesus talking,

> Therefore I say to you, do not worry about your life, what you will eat; nor about the body, what you will put on. Life is more than food, and the body is more than clothing. Consider the ravens, for they neither sow nor reap, which have neither storehouse nor barn and God feeds them. Of how much more value are you than the birds? (v.22-24)

Jesus' words cut straight to my heart. I looked over at Poppie. I sighed and smiled. I patted his thin, age-spotted arm. He smiled and patted my arm. He used to copy motions like that. As Pastor Chris spoke the red-letter words, I knew that Jesus didn't care that we were three hours off our morning routine, that we were watching the live stream, that we were absent from the church building, that Bob might not shave or brush his teeth that morning. This was a burden of perfection lifted. Chris continued:

> And which of you by worrying can add one cubit to his stature? If you then are not able to do the least, why are you anxious for the rest? Consider the lilies, how they grow: they neither toil nor spin; and yet I say to you, even Solomon in all his glory was not arrayed like one of these. (v.25-27)

How valuable must we be to our detail-oriented Creator who cares for ravens and lilies? As I type, I notice Calipari in my periphery, near the sunny window, no toiling, no spinning, just standing tall in the light and growing from its power. Changed. Being aware of God's presence is like spiritual photosynthesis. I purposefully sit still and breathe in and out slowly. The kangaroo part of me urged that I get a fly swatter and dash away the fruit flies. I resisted. More sitting. More breathing. More spiritual photosynthesis.

I looked down at my journal and my mind switched back to September:

> If then God so clothes the grass, which today is in the field and tomorrow is thrown into the oven, how much more will He clothe you, O you of little faith? And do not seek what you should eat or what you should drink, nor have an anxious mind. For all these things the nations of the world seek after, and your Father knows that you need these things. But seek the kingdom of God, and all these things shall be added to you. Do not fear, little flock, for it is your Father's good pleasure to give you the kingdom. (v.28-32)

Merriam-Webster defines anxiety as fear or nervousness about what might happen. Chris defined it this way: anything that hinders us, or drives us away, from intimacy with God. Both definitions imply doubt. Doubt is a feeling of indecision and uncertainty in conviction. Jesus exposed doubt's link to anxiety: He said, "you of little faith."

Is anxiety a universal experience? Probably. At the very least, we seem prone to it. As sophisticated as our world seems, we're anxious about the same things Jesus addressed two thousand years ago: our future: our food, our clothes, and ourselves: our looks and ability to make things happen, like adding a cubit to our stature. We get anxious when we think about ourselves. The inner voice cries out, "Me! Me! Me!" which further feeds the fear-doubt-worry-anxiety roller-coaster. Jesus knows our tendency to doubt. We doubt that God sees, knows, and cares about us. Perhaps doubt is based in a deep fear that God will neglect us. Jesus corrects gently (but clearly) with truth, "your Father knows that you need these things."

Even though Chris was preaching to the CrossBridge adults, he used props. You can count on youth pastors for props! Jackson, a senior high student, came forward with a small, single-shot Nerf® gun while Chris pulled out the multi-shot N-Strike Mega®. Chris aimed that huge toy gun and fired off a rapid sequence of foam darts representing an attack of lies from our spiritual enemy. The forces of darkness shoot us with a multi-shot weapon of false accusations and condemnations. Dark shades of deceit wound us from lies such as you're unloved, you're a burden, you're not wanted, you'll never amount to anything, you're less-than, you're not included, you're a freak. These lies are like rotten fruit, and anxiety emerges like unwelcomed, pesky fruit flies. How are there so many and where did they come from? What is the rotten source of their dishonest existence? Watching the live-stream, I clapped my hands and nodded, affirming my own experience of this cycle. I looked at Poppie. He nodded, too. Talking to the preacher on the laptop is one advantage of watching the livestream from home.

Chris fired off another round of Nerf® darts in Jackson's direction. He said that anxiety also develops in response to the world's multi-shot messaging weapon that we aren't enough, such as not good-looking enough, not smart enough, not rich enough, not capable enough, just not-enough-not-enough. Chris was giving examples of life's stressors that ring with and sting from the *not-enough* message: a note from your kid's teacher about a behavior concern, a harsh word or cold shoulder from a loved one, a work demand that exceeds your ability, an unmet expectation, a disappointing work performance review, and too many social media notifications from people bragging that they're better in every way. As the darts flew, the reality of how anxiety develops and overwhelms struck me.

Ill-equipped to fight off the mega-blaster, Jackson fired a single shot at Chris with his ridiculously too-small toy gun. In our own strength, we are powerless to fight off the attacks from our spiritual enemy, the accuser of the brethren, and the world of darkness. What can we do? Jesus gave three points of instruction.

First, consider the birds and the flowers. It's a satisfying meditation. I tried it; not in September at the counter with Poppie Bob, but just now, in my office as I read the sermon notes. I made my kangaroo-self sit still and breathe and pray. It worked. I even ignored the irritation of the pesky fruit flies.

Second, seek the Kingdom of God. Jesus revealed the link between the primary pursuit of self-satisfaction through earthly things and an anxious mind. *Seek the Kingdom* is advice to organize our priorities. Put God first. Don't worry, because all the other things we need will be provided. I thought about this directive. Something in me resisted the simplicity of it. I prayed through strong waves of doubt. After almost ten minutes, I experienced a breakthrough. The chattering static of incoming Me-Me-Me messages quieted underneath my focused awareness of God's perfect power. I visualized myself packing suitcases full of my concerns and then hauling those suitcases to the base of a large wooden cross where I stood and then kneeled. I could *be* weak and *feel* weak and then drag that weakness to the almighty source of strength, power, and love.

Third, do not fear. Chris emphasized this mandate in his Sunday sermon. I had a page and a half of notes scribbled down. Within Jesus' third anti-anxiety prescription, He calls us a sweet nickname and tells us *why* we need not worry: "Do not fear, little flock, for it is your Father's good pleasure to give you the kingdom." *Little flock* is a term of endearment used intentionally to demonstrate goodness and gentleness from God through Jesus. If we are His flock, He is the Good Shepherd. We are the sheep of His pasture. Just last week, Ellie, one of the life group girls, wanted prayer for her Vo-Ag (vocational agriculture) showcase. She was showing a sheep. Ellie said she can only handle caring for one since they are such anxious and frenzied creatures. They need contact with their caretaker to feel safe and settled.

Chris asked us to consider the love in the term, "little flock." He reminded us of the obvious. Nicknames aren't used when a parent is angry. Chris rattled off a string of sweet and clever nicknames for his wife and daughters. In my notes, (in black and blue ink), I wrote, "AnnaBanana, Bo-Didley, SG Dubb, SG Dog, Honey, NeelyBeth, Sweet Girls, and The Dillashaw Women."

We see who we are to God through the nickname "little flock." We are *His*. We are little in many ways and weak in many ways, too. But we are *His* flock. No flock is protected or powerful by the sheep's capabilities. Rather, it is the shepherd of the flock that has the power to provide and power to protect and the wisdom to lead and guide. The passage from Luke 12 is Jesus reminding us of truth which can be understood through the lens of the nickname, "little flock." Just like Ellie's little lamb, we too are safe and secure and less anxious and fretful when we are aware of the presence of our shepherd, Jesus Christ. Chris also pointed out that we are a *flock*, meaning we are meant to travel life's journey in the company of other sheep. Otherwise, we are prone to wander. As a pastor, Chris is an earthly shepherd and overseer, and often encourages us toward church community life.

Jesus told us that it was the Father's good pleasure to give us the kingdom. Chris broke this phrase down, but I can't make out from my messy notes what the Greek words were that he said. I have the words *"delight"* and *"bestow"* written down, maybe meaning that God is delighted to bestow to us the privilege of access to His kingdom. Chris said that we are children of a King which means we have access to heavenly treasures such as peace of mind, comfort in sadness, direction out of temptation, and hope in place of worry.

I'm glad I wrote these sermon notes, because it's really on this second reflection that I fully grasp the instruction in how to face anxiety. And since I have a strong kangaroo-type personality, I needed a second pass at this sermon. I see the source of unresolved emotions based on doubt that come from fear that God would neglect me. When I was little, like many little girls, I would pluck a daisy and pull the petals off one by one reciting the sing-song saying of "he loves me... he loves me not." I had a sudden realization that, in the crazy-making, anxiety-fostering way, I am prone to do that belief-unbelief game with God, especially when my external circumstances are disordered and chaotic, and my mind races in fear.

I'm thankful for Chris' spiritual definition of anxiety. I am committed to expose the things that block my intimacy with God. I see how believing the lies of the devil and the darkness of the world's system agitate me. I see how letting my agitations fester cause fermentation and belief rots into unbelief and steadfastness rots into indecisiveness and order rots into disorder.

Stringing Jesus' three-point action plan together, I sat in meditation, considering birds and flowers. I did an inner spiritual audit and mentally reprioritized. I smiled, knowing that I am counted as a sheep among God's little flock. And, in a gesture of faith to receive from a loving Father, I flung my hands open, palms up, and said, "I trust You, Lord." Calipari and I sat quietly in the light, changed by it, growing in it. Photosynthesis! Biological for *Cal* and spiritual for me!

Reflections & A Tune
And He has on a His robe and on His thigh a name written: KING OF KINGS AND LORD OF LORDS. (Revelation 19:16)
Even to them I will give in My house And within My walls a place and a name Better than that of sons and daughters; I will give them an everlasting name That shall not be cut off. (Isaiah 56:5)
My Father, who has given them to Me, is greater than all; and no one is able to snatch them out of My Father's hand. I and My Father are one. (John 10:29)
He who has an ear, let him hear what the Spirit says to the churches. To him who overcomes I will give some of the hidden manna to eat. And I will give him a white stone, and on the stone a new name written which no one knows except him who receives it. (Revelation 2:17)
Song recommendation: "Sparrows and Lilies" by Pat Barrett

Conversation Starters

- What are your nicknames? What about the nicknames of your family members?

- What things do you worry the most about?

- What would your life be like if you were free of anxiety?

- Do you have a real-life example of seeking first the Kingdom of God and then having things added to you?

Interview with Pastor Chris

Katie: Chris, do you mind if I ask you a few questions so we can add a little conversation to the end of our book?

Chris: Ask away.

Katie: Why is your ministry called *Ablaze*?

Chris: There is a verse in Romans (chapter 12:11) that encourages us to keep our hearts fervent (on fire) for the Lord and to serve Him. But, to tell you the truth, I didn't name the ministry. It was already named when I took the job.

Katie: Speaking of Romans, it's your favorite book of the Bible. Why?

Chris: Besides the gospels, I think Romans is the book that packs the biggest punch for giving us the doctrinal truths of a life with God. If all a person knew was what was written in the four gospels, he could go pretty far in his understanding if he also had the book of Romans. Romans has been a gauge for me in my own pursuit of holiness.

Katie: Do you have a second favorite book?

Chris: I'd have to say The Book of Psalms. I have drawn close to God by reading and studying the Psalms.

Katie: Where did you work before CrossBridge?

Chris: I was a traveling evangelist for SPM. I was gone from home a lot. At the time, Sarah Grace and Anna were little girls. I remember when Anna was about three years old and she didn't want me to leave her. We were at the airport saying goodbye. It really turned a page in my heart. Shortly after that I took the job with CrossBridge.

Katie: So, had you wanted to be a youth pastor?

Chris: (laughs) No way! I had no interest in youth. I felt I didn't relate to kids very well. CrossBridge had a vision for having a Family and Students Ministry Pastor, so that was how they sold it to me. When I took the job, I was only 28 years old. There were 27 students. Several, about 16, students left when I came on board. It was a slow start. (laughs again).

Katie: Wow! That must have been interesting. How many students do you have now? It must be close to two hundred from what I can tell.

Chris: Yes, there are about 150 students there each Wednesday, and about 215 students who are part of Ablaze.

Katie: Do you miss traveling and evangelizing in other countries?

Chris: I do, but I also have such a passion for students and families now so I can't imagine not doing what I do now. Plus, I still travel to other countries in the summers and share the Gospel.

Katie: If you didn't do youth ministry, what would you do?

Chris: I guess the only other thing I could see myself doing at this point is being a teaching pastor. I love to speak and teach the Word of God. It feels like my birthright. I also love the leadership role I have. I enjoy the youth ministry staff and the time I spend with them.

Katie: Do you have a typical way of writing sermons?

Chris: I follow a pretty standard format in that I always want to write so I can preach in an exegetical style.

Katie: Exegetical?

Chris: It's the fancy word that means I preach from the Scripture in a way to expound and teach the Word of God and what the Word means.

Katie: Is there another way to preach?

Chris: Yes. Some people preach from an idea or a topic and then find a Bible verse that fits with their message. I like to study the Word and break it down for students and the add my own stories to help make the passages come alive, or have meaning and current application.

Katie: So, how do you organize your sermons so you know what you're teaching?

Chris: I know what Bible texts I want to preach. Last year I wanted to teach the story of the Israelites leaving Egypt and so I made a series of sermons through the book of Exodus. I have a general outline or structure of the Scriptures and the concepts I want to teach each year. But, I follow the Holy Spirit's leading as I develop the specific plan.

Katie: How do you weave in the funny stories to keep things interesting for the students?

Chris: Well, I follow a few general guidelines. Like, I want to consider what the teenagers are feeling and the issues of the day, but I also don't want to only preach to address their feelings. Teenagers have many feelings! It's a little risky to have a funny or good story and then try to build a sermon out of it. I want to give students the Word of God and challenge them to a deeper understanding of the text. I do want to connect with the students so I will often share a story of my own life to keep them listening, but if I have a good story and it doesn't fit, I jot it down and file it and trust God that it will eventually fit in a sermon in some way, someday. I always want to preach to teens a message that points them in the direction of knowing who they are in Christ. I want them to know who Jesus is and that He is the One for them.

Katie: Do you have any other guidelines for writing your sermons?

Chris: I had a mentor give me an analogy once. He linked preaching to water skiing with a silly illustration that there will always be bodies in your wake. This was his funny way to tell me to stay covered in prayer and under the Lord's counsel to have the sermons do their intended work of feeding and growing the listeners.

Katie: Several times a year, you preach the Sunday morning sermon. Is that different for you, since you're used to preaching to teenagers?

Chris: It's not really that different in terms of preparing the messages. Well, except that with the teenagers, I am more liberal in telling a little story to gain or keep their attention, and when I am preaching to adults, I really make sure my stories link with the sermon. With the students, I am always connecting with them and asking myself what the students' greatest needs are.

Katie: You use great props when you preach. It's fun to have you preach on Sunday mornings because you make it fun and bring a youth pastor's enthusiasm to the message.

Chris: Thanks. I use entertainment to keep people's attention, and I have grown over the years in praying for the Holy Spirit to lead my sermons and then trusting that He will give me the right words to say.

Katie: I appreciate the time you must put in to making quality messages and teaching what the Scripture means.

Chris: Thanks. Oh, I've been thinking about an idea for another book.

Katie: Really? We started this book from an idea.

Chris: I know. It's almost been a year ago now.

Katie: A year goes by so fast. What is your idea?

Chris: I want to write about the mystery of how God communicates and expresses Himself through symbols and events and circumstances and people. I think it would help us understand Scripture more clearly and to see His hand at work in our own lives.

Katie: Interesting. Maybe should schedule a book meeting.

Chris: Yes. Let's.

Grace and Mercy: A Devotional Journey Playlist

Praise the LORD, for the LORD is good;
Sing praises to His name, for it is pleasant.

(Psalm 135:3)

Allow these songs to enrich your heart as you wash your mind in the truth of who you are in Christ.

"Old Church Choir" by Zach Williams (Chain Breaker, Essential Records, 2016)

"Hold Me Jesus" by Rich Mullins (Songs, Reunion, 1986)

"Directions" by Micah Tyler (Different, Fair Trade, 2016)

"My Story" by Big Daddy Weave (Beautiful Offerings, Fervent Records, 2015)

"Stand in Your Love" by Josh Baldwin (Without Words: Genesis, Bethel Music, 2019)

"Come to the Table" by Sidewalk Prophets (Something Different, Fervent Records, 2015)

"Never Stop Fighting for Me" by Riley Clemmons (Fighting For Me, Sparrow, 2019)

"Speak Life" by Toby Mac (Eye On It, ForeFront, 2012)

"Almost Home" by Mercy Me (Almost Home, Fair Trade, 2019)

"Known" by Tauren Wells (Hills and Valleys, Reunion, 2017)

"Come as You Are" by Crowder (Neon Steeple, Sparrow Records, 2014)

"The Way" by Pat Barrett (Pat Barrett, Bowyer & Bow, 2018)

"He Wears A Crown" by Bryan McCleery (He Wears A Crown- LIVE at CrossBridge, Watershed Music Group, 2019)

"O God Forgive Us" by For King & Country (Run Wild. Live Free. Love Strong., Fervent Records 2014).

"God of All My Days" by Casting Crowns (The Very Next Thing, Provident Music Group, 2016)

"Dead Man Walking" by Jeremy Camp (The Story's Not Over, Sparrow, 2019)

"Tell Your Heart to Beat Again" by Danny Gokey (Hope In Front of Me, BMG, 2014)

"God of This City" by Chris Tomlin (Hello Love, Sixsteps, 2008)

"I Have This Hope" by Tenth Avenue North (Followers, Reunion Records, 2016)

"How Can It Be?" by Lauren Daigle (How Can It Be, Centricity, 2015)

"Changed" by Jordan Feliz (Future, Centricity, 2018)

"Sparrows and Lilies" by Pat Barrett (Pat Barrett, Bowyer & Bow, 2018)

About the Authors

Kathleen ("Katie") Yancosek is originally from Kane, Pennsylvania. She lived in nine different cities before retiring from the Army in 2017 as a Lieutenant Colonel. She holds a bachelor's and a master's degree in occupational therapy and a PhD in rehabilitation science. Dr. Yancosek has co-authored 38 publications, including three book chapters. She co-authored *Handwriting for Heroes*, a six-week program on how to transfer hand dominance. Katie lives in San Antonio with her husband, Barry. They have two adult sons. Joshua, is serving in California with the U.S. Navy, and William is a college student at the University of Texas in Austin. Since her retirement, Katie is running a private rehabilitation practice to help people cope with neurological and behavioral health issues. In her free time she runs, reads, and writes. *Grace & Mercy: A Devotional Journey* was a unique partnership project between Katie and her pastor. Katie hopes this book will encourage personal growth in grace and mercy as well as bring people together around questions that matter. Katie's has two new book projects: one is a recovery workbook called *Recover in Color* and the other is a children's adventure book called *A Tale of Two Squirrels*.

Chris Dillashaw is the Student and Family Pastor at CrossBridge Community Church. Chris is a graduate of Baylor University with a degree in Religion. He has over twenty years in ministry and has been preaching since he was fifteen years old. He has a desire to see people connect to God's Word in real and practical ways. This creative partnership with Katie confirmed for Pastor Chris that preaching with stories doesn't just get a laugh, but actually helps people to connect with God through His Word. This book was an opportunity to witness the impact of sermon messages landing on the hearts of the listeners. Chris hopes that *Grace & Mercy — A Devotional Journey* will bless pastors and inspirational speakers. Chris is excited about the book's real-life application, and hopes that readers will develop a deeper love for God and the mystery of His revelatory Word. Chris has a heart for the nations and has evangelized in more than 25 countries. Chris is a native Texan and grew up in San Antonio. He and his wife, Ann Marie, have two daughters.

What's next for this pastor? Chris will be loving and serving Jesus with his whole heart and preaching every Wednesday night to his *Ablaze Ministry* students and to the entire CrossBridge congregation on selected Sundays. He will preach to anyone who will listen and respond... including goats!

CPSIA information can be obtained
at www.ICGtesting.com
Printed in the USA
BVHW070005100321
602118BV00005B/548